# STEAM TRAINS

The Magnificent History of Britain's
Locomotives from Stephenson's
*Rocket* to BR's *Evening Star*

# COLIN MAGGS

First published 2014
This edition published 2020

Amberley Publishing
The Hill, Stroud
Gloucestershire, GL5 4EP

www.amberley-books.com

ISBN 978 1 4456 9911 0 (paperback)
ISBN 978 1 4456 3283 4 (ebook)

Typeset by Fakenham Prepress Solutions, Fakenham, Norfolk NR21 8NN
Printed in Great Britain

# About the Author

Colin Maggs is one of the country's leading railway historians and has written over 100 books. In 1993 he received an MBE for services to railway history. His other great books include *A History of the Great Western Railway* ('Thoroughly researched and well written ... a very readable account of God's Wonderful Railway.' *BBC Who Do You Think You Are? Magazine*) and *The Train Driver's Manual*. He is currently writing a new biography of Isambard Kingdom Brunel, also for Amberley. He lives in Bath.

# Acknowledgements

Acknowledgement is due to Alan Dorrington for very helpful advice, while Gordon Dando and Colin Roberts also gave assistance.

# Contents

**MERSEY RAILWAY.**
For day of issue only. Not Transferable.

**3rd Class—Single.**
Issued subject to the Company's Regulations
and Conditions in their Time Tables.

**LIVERPOOL (CENTRAL)**
LOW LEVEL to
**JAMES STREET**
Fare 1ᵈ          B          9774

This Ticket is issued by the M.&D.R.
subject to the conditions stated on the
Co's Time Bills.

THIRD    CLASS

James Street          8810

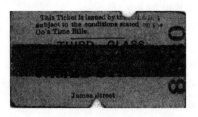

This Ticket is issued by the S.H.&D.R.
subject to the conditions stated on the
Co.'s Time Bills.

THIRD    CLASS

WEST KIRBY To
**NEW BRIGHTON**
Fare 8/-  West Kirby          3571

# 1

# Why Railways Were Developed and How the Steam Locomotive Was Invented

If you have the choice of walking along a rough path, or a smooth one, you will probably choose the latter because it is easier. Until relatively recently, roads were often rough and also boggy. Cartwheels tended to cut ruts in a road, and to obviate the problem of ruts men laid timber in them for carts to run on – rails had been invented. It was only with the increasing exploitation of minerals such as coal and iron ore, needed for the growing industrialisation of Britain, that an improved transport system, such as a railway, was essential.

One early English railway was at Wollaton, near Nottingham, and carried coal from pithead to navigable water. Regarding this, in 1610 the following was recorded:

> I beseche you to take order with Sir Thomas that we maie have libertie to bring coales down the railes by wagen, for our cariadges onely, and we will bring them down by raile ourselves, for Strelley cartway is so fowle as few cariadges can passe.

Construction was very simple: the cross sleepers were simply oak logs split in half, while the running rails were roughly squared and nailed to the sleepers with wooden pegs. The road was ballasted with earth or ashes, partly to protect it from the horses' hooves and partly to prevent the animals from tripping. Pits in Northumberland and Durham also used rails of timber, sometimes protected by thin iron plates as cast-iron wheels quickly wore out timber rails. The name 'rail' comes from rail-and-post fencing. Instead of drawing just one cart, on a railway a horse could pull four or five wagons.

In 1695 at Neath in South Wales, Sir Humphrey Mackworth ran 'the said Waggon-way on Wooden Railes from the face of each Wall of Coal twelve hundred yards under Ground quite down to the Water-side about three-quarters of a mile from the mouth of the Coal-pit'.

Another early example of such a line was Ralph Allen's railway opened at Bath in 1731 to carry stone from his quarries down to the River Avon. It descended on a gradient of 1 in 10, so loaded wagons could run down by gravity; they were drawn on the level, or uphill, by two horses. When houses were being built on the other side of the Avon, loaded trucks were carried across on barges – Ralph Allen had invented the train ferry. When constructing the Palladian Bridge below his home, to reach the bridge, a self-acting incline was built forming a branch line, a descending loaded wagon drawing up an empty one.

The 8-mile-long Tanfield line crossed Causey Burn by a stone bridge with an arch of 103 foot span designed by Ralph Wood, a local mason. He was so afraid his arch would collapse that he committed suicide, but his arch still stands today, bearing the inscription 'Ra. Wood, mason, 1727'.

The first railway in Scotland was a 2-mile line from coalpits at

Tranent to Cockenzie harbour, 10 miles east of Edinburgh, and this facilitated the coal-for-salt trade with Sweden. This line, later converted from timber to iron rails, remained in use for about 160 years.

The iron industry experienced a slump at the end of the Seven Years' War and in 1767 Coalbrookdale decided that, in order to keep the furnaces going, iron plates would be made to cover the timber rails of the local wagon way. The intention was to lift and melt them when trade improved, but as the wagons ran so much better than on timbers, these iron plates, 5 feet long, 4 inches wide and 1½ inches thick, were left in situ and more were cast. The rails were laid by platelayers, the name still used by today's permanent way men, but at what distance should rails be set apart?

A horse drawing a cart is placed between shafts and the width between the shafts is determined by the width of a horse's hindquarters. The width between the shafts determines the width of the wheels, and this was approximated to 4 feet 8½ inches. As it was intended that the plateways could be used by existing carts with flangeless wheels, the rail plates were edged on the inside to keep the wheels from wandering off the track.

When excavations were being carried out in the goods yard at Abbeydore station on the Golden Valley Railway, a Roman stone trackway was discovered which had distinct grooves in it, about 4½ feet apart.

John Curr, colliery agent at Sheffield, was probably the first to develop a cast-iron plateway with an inner flange on the rail. The plateway could take ordinary, flat-tyred road carts, but tended to get covered with stones, coal and dirt kicked up by horses, and this increased rolling resistance. To obviate the problem, William Jessop developed the cast-iron edge rail.

The invention also solved a difficulty as stagecoachmen strongly objected to his running flanged rails across the London-to-Derby turnpike road, so Jessop tried edge rail, which he sank in grooves where they crossed the road. His edged rail demanded flanged wheels. Although plateways continued to be laid until 1830, the coming of the locomotive doomed them as an edge rail can bear a much greater weight than a plate rail of the same weight and length.

The invention of the edge rail proved of vital importance. An L-section plateway could not be bent to form a curve, which meant that a curve had to be built with a series of tangents. The jerking motion when a wagon rounded a curve was no problem with the slow speed of horse traction, but it was a different matter with the greater speed of steam haulage. The shape of the I-section edge rail allowed it to be bent to a continuous curve, thus allowing rolling stock to round it smoothly.

In 1820, John Birkinshaw of Bedlington Iron Works, near Blyth, Northumberland, patented a roller mill for shaping malleable iron rails, which George Stephenson believed were better than those of cast iron. This machine was important because it took the manufacture of iron rails out of the hands of the iron founder and blacksmith and gave it to a power-driven machine that could turn out the vast numbers of rails which were soon to be needed.

For economy, the track was often single with passing loops within sight of each other, the rule being that if a train was approaching on a single line you waited at the loop for it to pass. If two trains chanced to meet head-on, the drivers fought to determine which should go back.

With industrialisation and the greater need for the transport of raw materials, finished goods and food supplies to urban areas, smooth roads were required so that a draught animal could draw a heavier load.

Although these horse railways were successful to a point, since a horse could draw two to three tons instead of half a ton on an ordinary road, or just 240 lb for a pack horse, they were not without their disadvantages – haulage power was limited and horses could become sick, particularly if disease spread in a stable. Thus the early railways were used either as feeders to waterways, where a horse could draw up to fifty tons on a canal, or for downhill loads where a canal would have been impracticable.

In 1803, the Surrey Iron Railway between Croydon and Wandsworth was the first public freight railway in the world; that is, it was open to anyone who paid the tolls. It was really a special sort of turnpike road, available for anyone who had a cart that could run on its rails and who could pay the toll. This ensured competition between carriers and therefore cheap rates to the public. In 1803, the last thing that a railway company was expected to do was to run trains. Notice the 'Iron' in its title – no old-fashioned timber rails for this new double-track plateway. Early railways were for carrying freight and mineral traffic, but in 1807 the railway from Oystermouth round Swansea Bay became the first public passenger line.

The landowners of the property crossed by these early railways charged way leaves at the rate of so much for each wagon and this provided them with a good income. In 1758, Charles Brandling was unable to get way leave for a 3½-mile-long railway from Middleton colliery across Hunslet Moor to Leeds. That year he overcame the difficulty by obtaining an Act of Parliament 'for the better supplying of the Town and Neighbourhood of Leeds, in the County of York, with coals'. This was the very first

Railway Act, and it stated where the railway was to run and what compensation was to be paid to landowners.

The first Scottish railway to obtain an Act of Parliament was the Kilmarnock & Troon Railway, a 10-mile plateway which opened in 1810 with horse traction and adopted locomotives in 1817.

# The First Locomotives

Horses had been used for pumping water from mines until James Watt and Matthew Boulton invented the steam engine. This worked not by steam pressure moving a piston, but by condensing steam creating a vacuum in a cylinder and the piston being forced down by air pressure.

Although such stationary engines were suitable for pumping water out of mines, they were too clumsy to be mobile as their design offered a low power-to-weight ratio and they were too heavy to carry themselves about.

Perhaps surprisingly, the first locomotive was not for railway use but ran on ordinary roads. It was made by William Murdock, who was born in Ayrshire on 21 August 1754. Employed by Boulton & Watt, in 1779 he was in Cornwall superintending the erection of James Watt's pumping engines.

Having an inventive mind, he turned his thoughts to producing a steam engine capable of moving. His first attempt was a model, rather than a full-size machine. A spirit-fired lamp raised steam in the boiler, which provided power to move a cylinder in a piston that moved up and down, driving the road wheels via a crank.

Having tested his locomotive indoors, he decided to carry out a longer test in the open air. Murdock believed it would be risky doing it in the daytime as it could frighten the town's residents, so opted to do it at night.

He took his locomotive to a narrow lane screened on each side by high hedges and then lit the spirit lamp. Steam was raised and, with the lamp flame shooting out of the short chimney, his engine moved off.

It accelerated rapidly and Murdock chased after it. The rector, on his way home, met this engine puffing and hissing along in an alarming and unearthly manner, and at first believed it to be a manifestation of the devil!

Murdock, pleased with his invention, set off to London intending to patent it. The first mention of Murdock's interest in a locomotive steam engine is in a letter of 7 March 1784 from Watt's agent in Cornwall to Watt:

> He [Murdock] has got an amazing genius and I am almost afraid will lead him too far. He has mentioned to me a new scheme which may be assured he is very interested upon but which he is afraid of mentioning to you for fear of you laughing at him, it is no less than drawing carriages upon the Road with Steam Engines ... He says that what he proposes, is different from anything you ever thought of, and that he is positively certain of its answering and that there is a great deal of Money to be made by it.

Matthew Boulton met him in Exeter and, alarmed at the possibility of the firm losing its best engineer, persuaded him to return to Cornwall. When he heard about the locomotive, the other partner, James Watt, was annoyed, considering such a machine impracticable. As such, Murdock made no further developments.

Richard Trevithick, son of a Cornish mine manager, eager to break Watt's stationary steam engine monopoly, developed the stationary engine worked by high-pressure steam. He used an engine with a double-acting cylinder, with steam admitted through a four-way valve and exhausted not through Watt's condenser but through a chimney. Trevithick's next development was using a boiler pressed to 45 lb/sq. inch, not the 14.7 of Newcomen & Watt. Trevithick's principle proved efficient and saved coal. His first steam carriage ran on Christmas Eve 1801 and travelled faster than walking pace. Between 1801 and 1803 he built three such vehicles, but the poor highway surface blocked further development. In the late 1820s and 1830s, Walter Hancock's and Goldsworthy Gurney's steam carriages achieved speeds of 20–30 mph, scaring both people and horses, while the Turnpike trusts, afraid of these vehicles damaging the road surface, charged excessive tolls.

# 2

# Locomotives Before the *Rocket*; the Important Move from Plate Rail to Edge Rail

On 13 February 1804, Trevithick ran his 0-4-0 railway locomotive, the very first in the world, on the line from Penydarren Ironworks, near Merthyr Tydfil, to Abercynon. It made the journey of 9½ miles in four hours and five minutes at an average speed of 2.4 mph. In addition to drawing ten tons of bar iron, it also hauled seventy sightseers and won a wager of 500 guineas. As it was a plateway, the wheels of Trevithick's engine would have had no flanges and could have run on an ordinary road had it been equipped with steering gear. Its boiler was about five feet in length, the single cylinder probably horizontal and on top of the boiler. It had a flywheel and the running wheels were driven by a train of gears. One of the striking features of the engine was that the exhaust steam from the cylinder was turned up the chimney, thus obtaining a forced draught and a consequent better drawing of the fire, a feature copied in all subsequent locomotives.

Although no problems were experienced regarding haulage as it satisfactorily drew ten tons over the 9½ miles, its weight of four tons fractured so many of the cast-iron plate rails that horse haulage was restored. Trevithick's second locomotive was for Wylam colliery, Northumberland, but the insubstantial wooden track prevented its use.

Trevithick's third locomotive, the 2-2-0 *Catch Me Who Can*, was, as its name suggests, more of a fairground venture. In 1808 it offered rides on a circular track near Euston, speeds reaching 15 mph. Better than the Penydarren engine, its vertical cylinder drove the wheels directly without the use of a flywheel. His use of a return-flue boiler and coupled wheels to improve adhesion were some of his ideas later developed by others.

At this point, Whyte's notation should be explained. F. M. Whyte, engineer of the New York Central Railroad, devised a useful system of explaining in shorthand what a particular locomotive looks like.

Basically, three figures show the wheels on one side of a locomotive starting from the front and indicating the leading, coupled and trailing wheels. In the event of no wheels appearing in a particular category, this is indicated by a nought – thus an engine with a four-wheeled bogie in front of six driving wheels is shown as a 4-6-0. Side tank engines are shown by the suffix 'T', with sub-division of 'PT' for 'pannier tank', 'ST' for 'saddle tank' and 'WT' for 'well tank'. A six-wheeled shunter would be classified as 0-6-0T.

In 1811, John Blenkinsop and Matthew Murray of the Middleton colliery obtained a patent for a steam locomotive propelled by a toothed wheel engaging in a rack on one of the rails. Unlike the previous one-cylinder engines, this 0-6-0 had two cylinders driving cranks set at right angles and proved to be the first commercially successful engine on any railway.

A Blenkinsop engine used by a Wigan colliery was described thus:

The people in the neighbourhood emphatically call it 'The Walking Horse' and certainly it bears no little resemblance to a living animal. The superabundant steam is emitted at each stroke with a noise something similar to the hard breathing or snorting of a horse – the escaping steam representing the breath of his nostrils, and the deception aided by the regular motion of the engine-beam.

The rack was found an unnecessary complication, and between 1813 and 1815 Thomas Hedley built three 0-4-0 locomotives with return-flue boilers and coupled wheels. As they experienced problems with broken plate rails, their weight was then distributed over eight wheels and successfully hauled fifty-ton loads on smooth rails. They were replaced by two four-wheelers, *Puffing Billy* and *Wylam Dilly*, Timothy Hackworth assisting Hedley. These ran on edge rails, which had superseded the plate variety as it was realised that there was little call for running ordinary road vehicles along a plateway. The first iron edge rails were made at Coalbrookdale, Shropshire, in 1767 and offered much less friction, allowing heavier loads to be drawn.

In 1811, Christopher Blackett, owner of Wylam Colliery, built a locomotive under the supervision of William Hedley. To economise on cost it had only one cylinder, but it was a case of 'cheap proving dear' and it was a failure. The following year, Hedley, Hackworth and Jonathan Foster, the latter being enginewright at Wylam colliery, built a two-cylinder locomotive. Although a mechanical success, it broke the tram plates. The problem was solved by placing it on two four-wheeled bogies to spread the weight.

In 1814, George Stephenson, who was born in a cottage beside the Wylam colliery railway, would have seen Hedley's engines. Stephenson, appointed enginewright of Killingsworth colliery in 1812, built his first locomotive, *Blucher*, named after the Prussian general and also a local colliery. Although able to draw a load of thirty tons up a gradient of 1 in 450 at 4 mph, it used a single-flue boiler rather than Trevithick's better return-flue design. *Blucher* proved rather prone to break down and could be difficult to start, on one occasion George Stephenson asking his sister-in-law to put her shoulder to the engine. Nevertheless, this locomotive impressed Edward Pearce, who was planning the 13-mile-long Stockton & Darlington Railway.

In 1825, George Stephenson invited Hackworth to be resident engineer to the Stockton & Darlington Railway. Hackworth lacked the business initiative of Stephenson, and Stephenson was good at appropriating the ideas of others. Hackworth improved Stephenson's locomotives by developing the blast pipe – whereby the exhaust drew fire through the boiler tubes – and used a return-flue boiler, both of which increased the available heating surface.

The result was the first steam-hauled public railway, which opened for goods only on 27 September 1825, Stephenson driving the 0-4-0 *Locomotion* that he designed and Hackworth improved, the wheels coupled by side rods rather than chains. George Stephenson was more notable as a civil engineer than as a locomotive designer. The engine was used only for goods, the railway company running a one-horse coach on the line which covered the distance between Stockton and Darlington faster than the four-in-hand coach on the turnpike road. In 1833, the company decided to take over all haulage and use steam exclusively.

In September 1827, *Royal George* appeared with further new features: six-coupled wheels for better adhesion, and four of these spring-mounted to give a more comfortable ride and offer less chance of derailment; a spring-loaded safety valve; self-lubricating bearings; and exhaust steam below the grate to stimulate combustion. In 1828, the Stockton & Darlington

Railway conveyed 22,442 tons for 22 miles by horse for £998, whereas the same load was carried over the same distance by *Royal George* for only £466.

The Somerset Coal Canal running south of Bath was served by a railway between collieries at Radstock and the canal at Midford. Three horses drew eight or nine wagons holding 1 ton 7 cwt each. The journey to Midford and back took five hours, which meant that two double trips could be made in a working day. At the height of the railway's fortunes, twenty-eight return trips were required daily.

In August 1826, William Ashman, engineer at Clandown colliery, one of the pits which supplied the line, built a steam locomotive which was able to draw nine loaded wagons between Clandown and Midford. It reached a speed of 3¾ mph on the level, but proved a failure owing to its weight of 2 tons 3 cwt breaking the cast-iron plates. Mechanically sound, it ended its days as a stationary engine at Clandown.

This Radstock line opened in 1815 was one of the first passenger-carrying lines in the country. On Saturdays, the coal wagons, known as 'tubs', were brushed out, boards were placed across them and they carried passengers from the villages en route to and from Radstock market.

Many of the early railways used stone sleeper blocks due to their rigidity and resistance to decay. Timber was considered a temporary expedient and some companies laid wooden sleepers on embankments and replaced them with stone blocks when the earthworks had consolidated. It was then found that the thrust of a locomotive's wheels tended to force the blocks out of gauge, so wooden cross sleepers were substituted, holding the rails firmly to gauge. In due course the rail joints were held together with fishplates, 'fish' being a nautical term for 'splint'.

The Liverpool & Manchester Railway underestimated the size of the rail required, and the 30 lb/yard rails of 1830 changed to 50, 60 and then 75 lb/yard in 1842.

George Stephenson had peculiar ideas about rail wear. He wrote,

> In the north the rails run longer than in the south, seeing that rails in the south dry quicker, being exposed to the sun's rays. It is well-known that all metallic surfaces wear much more when they are dry than wet, therefore presuming a line laid east to west and both rails wet, the south side of the rails will evidently dry sooner than the north side, the south side being immediately exposed to the sun's rays, while the north is defended therefrom by the upright edge of the rails, and therefore the north wheel will outrun that of the south.

Most of the early engineers preferred cast-iron rails to wrought because they corroded less easily. Wrought-iron rails tended to contain laminations due to impurities in the metal. Brunel recognised that this was a difficulty that would be overcome and that wrought iron rails held greater possibilities due to the greater lengths and variety of shapes in which they could be made. He designed a bridge rail for his 7 foot ¼ inch broad gauge, using an inverted 'U', weighing only 43 lb/yard as opposed to the 50 or 60 lb/yard of plain rail. He believed that his rail should be supported by a longitudinal sleeper as stone blocks were difficult to lay and required constant attention in order to be kept level, whereas his piles fixed the longitudinal sleepers securely.

Great Western director George Gibbs entered in his diary for 17 July 1838, when he rode on the London & Birmingham Railway, the following:

Their carriages and engines are much lighter than ours. The engines make much less noise and the general noise is less, but the wheels on the rails make more. The bumps or jolts at the joints are very frequent indeed, and are in some places very uncomfortable, and the joints show plainly the effects of the heavy blows they receive. The serpentine or lateral motion of which we have none on our railway is very striking; but on the other hand, they have no pitching or see-saw motion whatever, produced with us by the yielding of the timber between the piles.

These piles were removed or driven down deeper and riding of Great Western trains improved dramatically. With 62 lb/yard rails, his track designed for *North Star*, with a total weight of 23 tons – with about 11½ tons on the driving axle and a maximum speed of about 40 mph – was still capable of being utilised fifty years later by the large 4-2-2 engines, the most powerful engines on the broad gauge weighing 35½ tons and with 16 tons on the driving axle proceeding at 70 mph. The broad gauge ballast could be dug out in the centre of the 7-foot way to create a drainage channel, whereas with standard gauge this could prejudice the stability of the track.

Brunel's baulk road with longitudinal sleepers had undoubted advantages: no fishplates, no rail creep, no rail-end batter and, above all, an almost magically quiet ride. Its disadvantage was that locomotive crews found it gave 'dead riding' and drivers used to say that the engines were 'two coaches better' when travelling over transverse sleeper track.

Some companies using transverse sleeper track thought to economise by using rail of the double-bull-head pattern, so that the lower portion of the rails, which had been resting in chairs, could be turned over and become the top running surface when the original top surface had worn. The idea was found not to work: in their original position the chairs had made slight indentations into the rails, and after they had been turned over the effect of these was very strongly marked and produced a continual chattering sensation on the footplate, so the experiment was abandoned.

# 3

# The *Rocket*; Rainhill Trials; Why the *Rocket* Was so Good

The Liverpool & Manchester Railway was built to compete with the Bridgewater Canal, which had become inadequate for traffic and charged high tolls. It was said that sometimes it took less time to carry goods from America to Liverpool than to transport them by canal from Liverpool to Manchester!

By no means was everyone in favour of the line, as there were many against it: those who had invested in turnpike roads; coach proprietors; coach builders; saddlers and harness makers; and landowners who feared the presence of the railway would lower the value of their property and spoil their amenities.

The Liverpool & Manchester Railway was arguably the first major railway, with double track of iron rails, steam haulage for both passengers and goods and provision for first-, second- and third-class passengers. Lesser contenders are the Bolton & Leigh Railway, opened in 1828, and the Canterbury & Whitstable, opened four months before the Liverpool & Manchester on 3 May 1830. The Bolton & Leigh was really a feeder to the Leeds & Liverpool Canal and was worked by horse and steam, while the Canterbury & Whitstable was worked by stationary engines for two-thirds of its length.

Building a railway requires a wide variety of men with differing skills: lawyers, parliamentary agents, shareholders, stockbrokers and surveyors to initiate the company and then engineers, contractors and navvies to actually lay the track. Problems arose, such as the 30-foot-deep bog at Chat Moss. This was conquered by floating the railway on a raft of hurdles, brushwood and heather. At the Liverpool end of the line, a very deep cutting and tunnel were required. The pilot tunnel was up to 13 feet out of true, and an influx of water made it difficult to construct the masonry lining. As on the Stockton & Darlington, the Liverpool & Manchester Railway used wrought-iron rails laid on stone blocks, although wooden sleepers were employed over Chat Moss for lightness.

When planning a railway, a surveyor endeavoured to follow as flat a route as possible, because steam locomotives, not having gears, were relatively poor at climbing gradients. If a cutting or tunnel was required, the surveyor endeavoured to plan an embankment nearby to make use of the excavated spoil.

The navvies – named from the 'inland navigators' who built the canals – shovelled millions of tons of earth and rock, while miners excavated tunnels and their ventilation shafts and masons and bricklayers lined tunnels and built bridges. Each navvy lifted about 15 tons daily.

A full wagon was drawn from a cutting by a horse, and this horse was then replaced by a specially trained tipping horse who galloped to the temporary track before stepping smartly out of the way so that when the wagon of spoil struck a baulk at the end of the track, its contents shot out to lengthen the embankment.

Accidents and fatalities were all too common – falling rock and earth; being killed or injured by wagons; smoking near open gunpowder barrels or storing these barrels in a blacksmith's shop; or falling out of a large bucket when riding up the shaft out of a tunnel. Working in such conditions demanded relatively high pay, and it was not surprising that the navvies tended to get drunk and start fighting. Some 600 men were required to construct the Liverpool & Manchester Railway, although there were in excess of 250,000 navvies twenty years later, when railways were spreading over Britain; however, the average number at work between 1830 and 1870 was 50,000.

Railways required bridges across roads, rivers and canals and the Railway Clauses Act of 1845 decreed that an underline bridge should have a clearance in the centre of at least 16 feet for a turnpike road, 15 feet for an ordinary public road and 14 feet for a private road. The generous height was required to allow for top-hatted gentlemen riding on the outside of stagecoaches. Sometimes a road had to be dipped below a bridge to give sufficient clearance. Another important clause in the Act was that no railway could refuse to open its line to an independent branch line, provided that it did not run parallel with it.

With overline bridges, the height was 13 feet 6 inches from the rails. If a bridge had an approach embankment, the slope was not to exceed 1 in 30 for turnpike roads, 1 in 20 for other public roads and 1 in 16 for private roads. Although early bridges were generally of stone or brick, it was found that bridges of iron or steel girders could reduce by 2½ feet the distance from the road surface to the rails and thus did not require such long approach embankments.

Although Stephenson was a locomotive enthusiast, it was not a foregone conclusion that his favourite motive power would be used, some Liverpool & Manchester directors believing a stationary engine and cable haulage to be more reliable. A stationary engine was indeed used for the Edgehill Tunnel incline and a competition held for finding the best locomotive, a £500 prize being offered for an engine weighing less than 4½ tons which could haul three times its own weight for 70 miles at an average speed of not less than 10 mph and which would cost no more than £550. These trials were to take place at Rainhill, midway along the line.

In the competition, engines were required to travel to and fro over a trial length of 1¾ miles to equal a distance of 35 miles – the distance between Liverpool and Manchester. Later in the trials, the judges increased this distance to 70 miles. Although ten locomotives were entered, only five began the test on 6 October 1829.

The *Liverpool Courier* recorded on 7 October 1829 that 'never, perhaps, on any previous occasion, were so many scientific gentlemen and practical engineers collected together on one spot'. Joseph Locke, President of the Institution of Civil Engineers, likened the trials to the St Leger, with tents for ladies, a band to entertain and stands for spectators. There were three main contestants: Robert Stephenson's 0-2-2 *Rocket*, the 2-2-0 *Novelty* of Messrs Braithwaite & Ericsson and the 0-4-0 *Sans Pareil* of Timothy Hackworth. *Rocket* was broken down and crated, then travelled by horse and cart from Newcastle to Carlisle and then by canal to Bowness-on-Solway, where the crates were loaded on to a boat to carry them to Liverpool.

The other two engines were *Perseverance*, built by Timothy Burstall of Leigh, which had to be disqualified as it only reached 5 mph, and *The Cycloped*, powered by a horse.

*Rocket* and *Novelty* reached a speed of 30 mph and caused great excitement among the crowd of at least 10,000, plus 200 men acting as special constables. An eyewitness wrote of *Rocket*:

It seemed indeed to fly, presenting one of the most sublime spectacles of mechanical ingenuity and human daring the world ever beheld. It actually made one giddy to look at it, and filled the breasts of thousands with lively fears for the safety of the individuals who were on it, and who seemed not to run along the earth, but to fly, as it were, 'on the wings of wind'.

Messrs Braithwaite & Ericsson's *Novelty* performed well on 6 October, but suffered a broken pipe on the 10th. The trial was spread over seven days.

The winner was Stephenson's *Rocket*, decked out in a livery of canary yellow and white, which proved the only machine to complete the course successfully. It averaged 16 mph and was capable of exceeding a maximum of over 30 mph.

This engine, instead of having one large flue through the boiler, had twenty-five small copper tubes, an idea suggested by Henry Booth, the Liverpool & Manchester's treasurer, who knew of the invention by the Frenchman Marc Seguin. This improvement considerably increased its heating area, thus making the machine more efficient. Another development was that the pipe exhausting steam from the cylinders was designed to draw heat through these tubes. The secret of Hackworth's blast pipe was discovered one night on a surreptitious inspection of a rival locomotive, the 0-4-0 *Sans Pareil* entered by Hackworth.

It is sad to record that, during the Rainhill Trials, *Sans Pareil* burst a cylinder due to the faulty workmanship of its builders – Messrs Stephenson, no less. The cylinder wall was only a sixteenth of an inch thick instead of seven-eighths! Ironically, when *Sans Pareil* was repaired following the trials, she proved superior to the *Rocket*. Later improvements to *Rocket* added a water jacket round the firebox to increase steam production and a smoke box to collect char. Hackworth's *Globe* was the first engine to have a dome in order to collect dry steam, which made an engine more efficient. An engineer named John Dixon wrote, 'The *Rocket* is by far the best Engine I have ever seen.' He said that *Sans Pareil* was 'very ugly' and that *Novelty* was like a 'Tea Urn with a Parlour-like appearance'.

After the prize of £500 was presented to the owners and designer of *Rocket*, four more of the same class were ordered for the Liverpool & Manchester.

It could be said that far too much importance has been given to George Stephenson's influence on locomotives. This was due to his biographer, Samuel Smiles, enjoying making him rise from obscurity to become a household name. George Stephenson's gift was adapting the ideas of others.

The opening of the Liverpool & Manchester Railway on 15 September 1830 marked the first serious railway fatality. William Huskisson, leader of the progressive wing of the Tories, was killed. The engine of his train had stopped to take water at Parkside and Huskisson took the opportunity to get out and stretch his legs. *Rocket* approached, and, when returning to his coach, he fell and his leg was crushed under *Rocket*'s wheels. *Northumbrian* was coupled to a single coach and Huskisson rushed to Eccles at 36 mph, but he died at the vicarage there. That day, the eight special trains carried a total of over a thousand passengers. The *Northumbrian* was the first locomotive to have a proper tender as opposed to a coal cart-cum-water barrel.

For many years, the locomotive department of the early railways had to carry out improvements to meet the requirements of increasingly heavy traffic: iron wheels were substituted for wooden, crank axles were formed with almost double the amount of metal, and likewise pistons, piston rods and connecting rods were strengthened. Alterations involved an augmentation of weight so that the 4½ tons of *Rocket* was increased to the 10 tons of the Planet class. The *Planet* had inside cylinders placed at the front of the frames, a feature copied by most subsequent engines for the next fifty years.

An outstanding value of the railway, apart from its speed, was that it greatly reduced the cost of travel. Coach fares between Liverpool and Manchester were 5s 0d outside and 10s 0d inside, but railways reduced this to only 3s 6d outside and 5s 0d inside. Before the opening of the railway, goods between Liverpool and Manchester were charged about 18s 0d a ton, but the railway reduced this to less than 10s 0d; and instead of paying £5 a ton for the transport of bale goods between Manchester and London, a merchant using the railway paid less than £1 10s 0d. Sir James Allport, manager of the Midland Railway, said that with the coming of the railway people in London were paying less for coal than they had paid for just for its carriage before railways came into operation.

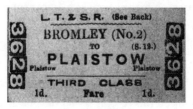

**L. T. & S. R.** (See Back)

**BROMLEY (No.2)**

TO      (S. 13.)

**PLAISTOW**

Plaistow          Plaistow

**THIRD CLASS**

1d.      Fare      1d.

3628     3628

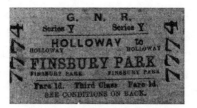

**G. N. R.**

Series **Y**      Series **Y**

**HOLLOWAY** to

HOLLOWAY        HOLLOWAY

**FINSBURY PARK**

FINSBURY PARK      FINSBURY PARK

Fare 1d.   Third Class   Fare 1d.

SEE CONDITIONS ON BACK.

7774     7774

**LANC. & YORK. RLY.**

Issued subject to the Regulations and Conditions in the Co's Time Table, Book Bills and Notices. Available for ONE Journey only on day of issue or following day.

THIRD CLASS

**Lostock Jun**

To

**WESTHOUGHTON**

16 1

Lostoc

# 4

# Early Railways in Great Britain

October 1830 saw the appearance of Robert Stephenson's 2-2-0 *Planet*, the ancestor of subsequent steam locomotives. Rather than the cylinders being hung on the outside of the boiler in an ungainly fashion, they were tucked neatly beneath the smoke box and between the frames, where they were kept snug and warm. This prevented the condensation of steam in the cylinders and the consequent loss of power. A further novel feature of the 2-2-0 *Planet* was that it had the firebox inside the boiler instead of at the end.

A journalist wrote that the fact that the thirty miles from Liverpool to Manchester could be achieved in an hour was evidence of an extraordinary increase in both the power and efficiency of this locomotive, as compared with its predecessors. Having inside cylinders necessitated a crank-axle drive, which was more complicated to make. The following year, Robert Stephenson built *Goliath*, a 0-4-0 version for coping with the incline out of Liverpool.

The 6-mile-long Canterbury & Whitstable Railway received its Act in 1825. This short line had no less than four methods of haulage: fixed engine, gravity, locomotive and horse. Its locomotive, the 0-4-0 *Invicta*, was purchased from Robert Stephenson's factory for £635.

The next London line after the Surrey Iron Railway was the London & Greenwich Railway, opened to Deptford in 1836 and reaching Greenwich two years later. The most remarkable thing about the line was that it ran for practically the whole of its 3¾ miles on a viaduct of brick arches designed by Col G. T. Landmann. Although expensive to construct, it took up less space than an embankment and was less of an obstacle to roads. Moreover, as an early Victorian writer observed, 'the vacant spaces beneath the arches may be let for tenements, shops, warehouses, or fitted up as ragged schools'.

Initially the line was exhibited as a show and special attractions offered, such as a band of musicians dressed as Beefeaters stationed at its London terminus and another band at Deptford. For the sake of economy, the Deptford band was soon replaced by a large barrel organ which welcomed passengers, but when traffic became established these delights were withdrawn. Initially the line was lit at night by a row of lamps on each side, but eventually this was discontinued as unnecessary. During the first eleven months the line carried 456,750 passengers, or a daily average of about 1,300.

North of the Thames, the London & Blackwall Railway linked the City with the West India and East India Docks. Of 5-foot gauge, it had rope haulage by stationary engines. This elevated line was eventually extended westwards to Fenchurch Street, where one has to go upstairs to catch a train. The buildings that now hide much of the viaducts were not there when these two lines were made.

The year 1833 saw the appearance of Stephenson's *Patentee*. There were two versions: an inside-cylinder 2-2-2 for passenger duty and a 0-4-2 for goods. Its cylinders were placed inside the frame under the smoke box, thus keeping them warm and also giving the locomotive a better balance as outside-cylinder locomotives tend to waddle. A later example of a Liverpool & Manchester engine exists in the 0-4-2 *Lion*, star of the film *The Titfield Thunderbolt*. On the Leicester & Swannington, some of the Patentee goods engines had the wheels on the trailing axle coupled, thus turning them into 0-6-0s.

An important development in 1842 was Stephenson's link motion, though it was actually invented by William Howe, a patternmaker for Stephenson. This system allowed a driver to progressively decrease the amount of steam admitted to the cylinders, thus allowing the steam more time to expand and therefore saving fuel. Steam was admitted for 75–80 per cent of the piston stroke when starting, but only 10–15 per cent when it was only necessary to maintain the speed reached.

Early engines tended to have either the 2-2-2, 2-2-0 or 0-2-2 wheel arrangement for passenger working – uncoupled wheels offering smoother running, especially at speed – but goods trains, being generally heavier, required coupled wheels such as 0-4-0 or 0-6-0 in order to provide the necessary adhesion. Six wheels were essential when increased power was demanded, because when the strength of the rails was limited an increase from four to six wheels was needed in order to distribute the extra weight.

The basic characteristics of a steam locomotive had now been cast and would remain, with relatively minor improvements, until the end of general steam working:

1. Two cylinders, with cranks set at right angles (unless three- or four-cylindered).
2. Blast-pipe exhaust.
3. Multi-tube boiler.

4. Valve to control the admission of steam for only part of a stroke.

In 1842, the Great Western's North Star class 2-2-2 locomotives cost about £2,000 each plus £500 for a tender. In 1875, the same company was able to dispose, mainly for stationary use, of sixty-three redundant broad gauge engines for £500 each and twenty-eight tenders at £50 each.

Elderly locomotives can be put to other uses: the workshops at Swindon at one time had machinery driven by old engines, and they could also be used to drive air compressors for pneumatic riveting on bridges. Even old tenders had their use: the Great Western decided to celebrate Queen Victoria's Jubilee in 1887 with tea in the railway park, and the locomotive department was given the task of making the tea.

The original idea was to empty tea chests into tenders filled with cold water and then turn steam from an engine into them. This idea was modified. Some tenders were cleaned out, the man deputed to do the job coming out in about ten seconds with the remark that, if tea was to be made in those tanks, he would turn over a new leaf and drink beer for the rest of his life!

Eventually placed in a fair state of cleanliness, taps were fitted in the side of the tenders, steam blown in to get the water at boiling point, and then tea urns were filled from the taps. In the following days, Swindon doctors had no more cases to deal with than usual.

With Liverpool and Manchester having been linked by rail, other major cities now wished to be linked by this new form of transport.

The Grand Junction Railway received its Act in 1833 to build a line from a junction with the Liverpool & Manchester Railway at Earlestown to a station at Curzon Street, Birmingham, alongside that of the proposed London & Birmingham Railway. George Stephenson was the engineer, with Joseph Locke as deputy. However, as the latter did most of the work, the directors, disliking Stephenson's lack of interest, made Locke chief engineer. The line had relatively few heavy engineering works and was a credit to Locke as it was built on time and within the budget.

It was the Grand Junction which introduced the travelling post office to the world. F. Karstadt, son of a Post Office surveyor of German extraction, suggested that time could be saved by sorting letters during the journey. On 6 January 1838, a sorting carriage adapted from a Grand Junction horsebox entered service between Birmingham and Liverpool. By May a folding net had been devised to pick up pouches at speed, a similar apparatus delivering them to the lineside.

The first major railway to appoint George Stephenson's son, Robert, as engineer was the London & Birmingham. The 112-mile-long line was authorised by Parliament in 1833, on the same day as the Grand Junction Railway. It was originally planned to have Camden as its southern terminus in order to avoid an incline of 1 in 70, but then it was decided to bring it nearer to the City and make Euston the terminus. Too large an undertaking to be opened in its entirety, the railway was opened in stages between 1837 and 1838.

The line had eight tunnels, of which Kilsby, south of Rugby, proved the most difficult to cut due to the problem of dealing with running sand. Deep cuttings had to be made at Tring and Roade to enable the line northwards from Camden, with a ruling gradient of 1 in 300. Until 1844, the 1¼-mile-long incline between Euston and Camden was operated by cable and stationary winding engines.

John Britton, writing in Bourne's *London & Birmingham*

*Railway*, published in 1839, describes the dangerous work of a navvy creating a cutting:

> The horse, in moving along the top of the embankment, draws the rope attached to a wheelbarrow round two pulleys, and thereby raises the barrow of earth up the sloping board, together with the labourer who holds and guides it. This is a dangerous occupation, for the man rather hangs to, rather that supports the barrow, which is rendered unmanageable by the least irregularity in the horse's motion. If he finds himself unable to govern it, he endeavours, by a sudden jerk, to raise himself erect; then, throwing the barrow over one side of the board, or 'run', he swings himself round and runs down the other. Should both fall on the same side, his best speed is necessary to escape the barrow, which, with its contents, comes bounding down after him. Although there were from thirty to forty horse runs in the Tring cutting constantly working, during many months, each labourer was precipitated down the slopes several times; such, from continual practice, was their sure-footedness, that only one fatal accident occurred. A moving platform was invented by the engineer to supersede the necessity of thus risking life and limb, but the workmen, who considered it was designed to lessen their labour, and wages, broke it.

Navvies were relatively well paid, receiving some 15s a week compared with a farm labourer's wage of 10s. Navvies, however, often had to purchase food in shops run by railway contractors, where prices were 10 per cent above the market rate. Often living in squalid huts, it is not surprising that navvies drank to excess on pay days, though they were always polite and respectful towards missionaries, who looked after their spiritual welfare. When the pay days of English and Irish labourers engaged on the Lancaster and Carlisle line took place, it was several times found necessary to keep a regiment of infantry and a troop of yeomanry cavalry in readiness to prevent dangerous and perhaps fatal riots.

Although of necessity their weekday clothes were not smart, on Sundays and holidays many of the navvies were 'resplendent in scarlet of yellow or blue plush waistcoats and knee breeches' (Creswell, *Winchmore Hill*, 1912).

Navvies took pride in their work. Just north of Bugsworth station on the Ambergate and Manchester line was a tunnel, and one day part fell in, trapping some men. A shaft was sunk through which they hoped the men could be liberated, and, after twenty-three hours of hard work in relays, they were reached. When they were found, lying exhausted from want of air, it was learned that when the tunnel collapsed one of the men had said to the others, 'Well, chaps, we'll never get out alive, so we may as well get on with "our bit" while we can.' And they went on till they could go on no longer.

As there was insufficient room to slope the sides of Camden cutting to prevent a landslide, Stephenson lined it with thick brick walls. Charles Dickens lived in Camden Town at that time, and in *Dombey & Son* he vividly describes the chaos caused by the line's construction.

To give early railway travellers confidence, a great Doric portico designed by Philip Hardwick was built at Euston, giving clear indication that this was the Gateway to the North and that the railway was the road of the future. Birmingham had a corresponding Ionic counterpart alongside the Grand Junction Railway's terminus.

In the line's early days, when approached to allow the transport of coal, one of the directors exclaimed that there was but one lower depth to which his railway could sink – that of carrying dung! Even when consent was given for the transport of coal, a high screen was erected between the line and the Grand Junction Canal wharf at Weedon, where it was transhipped from barges into the railway wagons, in order to hide the operation from the scandalised eyes of passing passengers; the wagons were sheeted over for the same reason.

The London & Birmingham and the Grand Junction Railway amalgamated in 1846, becoming the London & North Western Railway.

The Leeds & Selby Railway opened in 1834 and carried coal from the Garforth mines to the navigable Ouse at Selby. In 1840, the Hull & Selby carried traffic to the Humber. The Leeds & Selby was the first company to purchase enough land for quadruple tracks, though, in the event, two lines sufficed.

In the meantime, railways were being developed in Scotland. The first railway in Scotland was the Tranent waggonway, opened in 1722 to carry coal 2 miles from the Tranent mines to ships at Cockenzie. Set on stone sleeper blocks, the wooden rails had a gauge of 3 feet 3 inches. It was no accident that Scotland's excellent education system provided such eminent engineers as Dugald Drummond, John Macadam, Walter Neilson, Patrick Stirling, Thomas Telford and James Watt. In 1766, a line was opened between Kinnaird colliery and blast furnaces at Falkirk. Rails were initially of wood protected by thin strips of iron, but the following year these were replaced by cast-iron rails from Coalbrookdale.

The Garnkirk & Glasgow, which opened in 1831, used steam and horse haulage, but this was just a local line. Its two locomotives, not of the latest design, were supplied by George Stephenson. When the Monkland & Kirkintilloch changed from horse to locomotive power it met a problem – a low tunnel did not offer sufficient headroom. The temporary expedient was adopted of one engine working north of the tunnel and the other to the south, horses drawing traffic through the tunnel. Following the opening out of the tunnel in January 1832, allowing through working, loaded trains proceeded down the line at 5 mph and returned with empties at 2–3 mph, George Dodds, the company engineer, explaining to the directors that the new engines went slowly as higher speeds would cause wear and tear 'and moreover hurt the coals'.

In due course, the Monkland & Kirkintilloch doubled its line. A problem then arose due to 1½ miles of line being used by the Garnkirk & Glasgow, which still used much horse traction, and careless drivers detached horses and allowed wagons to run into and damage Monkland & Kirkintilloch locomotives. The problem was solved by working the double line as two single lines – one for horse-drawn traffic and the other for steam.

At one point, a passenger train on the Ballochney Railway, which fed the Monkland & Kirkintilloch, was drawn up a self-acting incline by loaded coal wagons descending a parallel track. An accident occurred on 28 October 1846 when the rope broke and coaches and coal wagons plunged down to pile in a heap at the foot of the incline.

On 15 July 1837, the Glasgow, Paisley, Kilmarnock & Ayr and the Glasgow, Paisley & Greenock Railway companies received their Acts, while the Edinburgh & Glasgow Railway received its authority in 1838. They opened in 1840, 1841 and 1842 respectively. There was certainly scope for railways serving the Clyde, as steamer services were so dense that paddle steamers were forced to berth at an angle to the quay wall; in 1838 and 1839, no less than sixty-nine collisions between vessels were recorded.

The opening of the Glasgow, Paisley, Kilmarnock & Ayr

enabled the first West Coast service to be inaugurated between Glasgow and London. On alternate weekdays, a fast steamer, the *Fire King*, sailed from Ardrossan to Liverpool and vice versa. She connected with the London expresses of the Grand Junction and the London & Birmingham and a special boat train was run between Glasgow and Ardrossan.

The Edinburgh & Glasgow was engineered as a high-speed line, cuttings, embankments, tunnels and viaducts rendering the line virtually level, the greatest engineering feature being Robert Telford's thirty-six-arch viaduct across the Almond Valley. The exception to the flat route was Cowlairs incline, 1½ miles of 1 in 41 leading down through a tunnel to Glasgow, Queen Street. Locomotives and their trains were hauled up by a stationary steam engine but descended engineless, with special brake wagons attached. Locomotives assisted the stationary haulage engine, and the dexterity with which the locomotives slipped the cable at Cowlairs without stopping was one of the sights of Glasgow. The station was so close to the tunnel mouth that sometimes, with a long train, passengers had to squeeze through the narrow space between the sooty tunnel wall and the coaches to reach their seats. In 1844, locomotive superintendent William Paton designed two six-coupled banking engines, at the time the most powerful in the country. Unfortunately they damaged the track, so rope haulage continued until 1908. Paton was unfortunate, as he received a year's prison sentence for culpable homicide following a boiler explosion.

Scotland demanded a railway link to England, just as England required a link to Scotland. By 1850, there were three Anglo-Scottish routes. Two followed the West Coast: the Glasgow & South Western, which had been formed by the amalgamation of the Glasgow, Paisley, Kilmarnock & Ayr and the Glasgow, Dumfries & Carlisle; and the Caledonian from Glasgow and

Edinburgh to Carstairs and Carlisle. The North British provided the East Coast route from Berwick to Edinburgh.

The first railway route from Edinburgh and Glasgow to London was completed in 1848. This West Coast route was operated by the Caledonian and the London & North Western. The East Coast route was opened in 1852 by the North British, North Eastern and the Great Northern.

Travelling northwards, Aberdeen was reached in April 1850, resulting in the loss of eight minutes and twenty-two seconds when GMT replaced local time to facilitate timetabling.

Wick and Thurso were a further 161 miles, this being 2.78 times the direct distance to Wick and 1.23 times the distance by road. The line opened to Dingwall on 11 June 1862 and eventually reached Wick and Thurso on 28 July 1874.

Speed on the Highland line could not always be expected. Early in the twentieth century, E. L. Ahrons recorded in the *Railway Magazine* recollections of the previous century:

Passengers could get through from Wick to Perth if they liked to spend much time in doing it. This left Wick at 11.30 a.m., and arrived at Inverness at 7.35 p.m., where they could wait and have dinner before leaving by the south-bound train at 10.00 p.m., to reach Perth at 7.10 a.m., in time for breakfast.

But Sunday being the Sabbath, the Highlanders thought the best thing to do with the Up mail train from Wick would be to knock some two hours off its schedule time, and consequently curtail the amount of desecration required in running it on that day. So instead of leaving Wick at 12.10 a.m., it did not depart until 2.30 a.m., but nevertheless arrived at Inverness at 9.50 a.m., only fifteen minutes later than its weekday arrival. Truly the Sabbath had its advantages to Caithnesshire.

Snow caused problems, in 1881 causing the line between Inverness and Perth to be closed for six weeks. Matters were later improved by the erection of snow fences comprising old sleepers driven vertically into the ground at spots susceptible to drifting. A snowblower was installed on the boundary of Caithness and Sutherland. This was a kind of leaning fence set on both sides of the track, and closest to the rails it was just a few inches off the ground, while the outer edge was 8–10 feet high. This caused the wind to deflect snow away from the track.

Some of the Scottish trains were amazing in both length and composition. E. Foxwell, in *Express Trains, English and Foreign*, published in 1888, wrote regarding an express from Perth:

In July and August the 7.50 a.m. train is the unique railway phenomenon. Passenger carriages, saloons, horse-boxes and vans, concentrated at Perth from all parts of England, and intermixed to make an irregular caravan. Engines attached fore and aft and the procession toils pluckily over the Grampians. Thus on August 7th, 1888, this train sailed out of Perth composed as follows:

| | |
|---|---|
| London, Brighton & South Coast Railway | Horse-box |
| do | do |
| do | Carriage van |
| do | Horse-box |
| London & North Western Railway | Horse-box |
| North Eastern Railway | Horse-box |
| London & North Western Railway | Saloon |
| do | Horse-box |
| Midland Railway | Saloon |
| do | Luggage van |
| do | Carriage truck |

| | |
|---|---|
| do | Horse-box |
| London & North Western Railway | Horse-box |
| North British Railway | Luggage van |
| do | Horse-box |
| do | Horse-box |
| do | Horse-box |
| East Coast Joint Stock | Sleeping car |
| Great Northern Railway | Saloon |
| West Coast Joint Stock | Composite |
| Midland Railway | Composite |
| London & North Western Railway | Luggage van |
| London & South Western Railway | Horse-box |
| West Coast Joint Stock | Composite |
| London & North Western Railway | Horse-box |
| do | Meat van |
| Highland Railway | Post Office van |
| do | Luggage van |
| do | Third class passenger |
| do | First class passenger |
| do | Second class passenger |
| do | Third class passenger |
| do | Luggage van |
| do | Third class passenger |
| do | First class passenger |
| do | Third class passenger |
| do | Guard's van |

A total of nine railway companies were involved and thirty-six carriages, with two engines in front and one placed behind at Blair Atholl. It left Perth twenty minutes late, and Kingussie seventy-two minutes late.

Commenting in his delightful manner, Ahrons said that he was not sure whether the Highland Railway was not transgressing a Board of Trade regulation:

Writing from memory I think that a rule was made about the year 1884 to the effect that no passenger train was to exceed an amount of stock equivalent to 20 six-wheeled coaches. But then the Board of Trade spent much time in making rules and regulations, some of which might possibly have been carried out on a large English railway, but which were utterly impossible when application of them was intended for a line like the Highland. Consequently the latter Company spent an equal amount of time in breaking or evading the impossible conundrums which the Whitehall wiseacres set them, for had any attempt been made to carry them out, traffic on the Highland would have come to a dead stop.

Amongst other things to which the Board of Trade objected was the use of a banking engine behind the train, and they wanted a pilot engine in front. The Highland did both; on such trains as the one just described the Board of Trade got its pilot engine in front, and the Highland put its 'banker' behind and completed the edifice. However the Board had the pleasure of making regulations, and the Highland authorities read them and carried on their 'business as usual,' so everybody was satisfied.

W. M. Acworth, in *The Railways of Scotland*, published in 1890, was scathing in his remarks on the operation of the Highland Railway:

It ignores the block system, it will have nothing to do with train staff or train tablet, but works its traffic (as also its neighbour the Great North in most parts) on the old-fashioned system of telegraphic crossing orders; its facing points are often unprovided with locking bars, in some cases they are not even interlocked with the signals. Most of its trains are mixed, some of them are very mixed indeed, and the passenger carriages are always in the rear. I came into Inverness not long since from the north in a train of 35 goods trucks followed by seven passenger coaches.

The fact of having goods wagons at the front meant that the passenger coaches did not have the benefit of continuous brakes, so that in the event of a breakaway they would not automatically be stopped. Having loose coupled wagons in the train would produce a jerky ride on starting and stopping as the buffers drew apart and then bumped together. In 1889, the Board of Trade required passenger coaches to be marshalled next to the engine.

The Duke of Sutherland, who was the driving force behind the construction of the Wick and Thurso line, had his own private station at Dunrobin, where he kept his own saloon and locomotive, which he personally drove over the lines of other companies. With the Amalgamation in 1923, the London, Midland & Scottish Railway continued to uphold this arrangement, but it came to an end when the railways were nationalised in 1948.

In 1899, the London & North Western Railway, of which he was a director, built him a larger saloon and this was the prototype for the royal train built four years later. The duke was the only owner of a private railway carriage in the British Isles.

The Great North of Scotland Railway made an innovation copied by other companies. Tank engines suffered from severe draughts which blew round the footplate due to the wind caught by the bunker front being reflected back on the crew. To prevent this, the locomotive superintendent, James Manson, fitted his new tank engines with simple hinged iron doors which could be closed when running. As soon as he heard of them, S. W. Johnson of the Midland fitted all his 0-4-4Ts with similar doors and many other lines adopted this improvement and also applied it to their tender engines.

The railway pattern of Wales is rather different from that of England and Scotland. Although it possessed some of the earliest railways in Britain, they were local lines carrying mineral traffic from pits to the sea, there being less enthusiasm for creating trunk lines for use within the principality; in fact, the two Welsh main lines were really aimed at carrying through traffic from London to Ireland. The Chester & Holyhead opened in 1851 along the north coast, and in 1856 the South Wales Railway opened along the south coast to Milford Haven. What was missing, and indeed is still missing, was a main line linking North and South Wales – the only route now available is that following the border between Wales and England.

English companies promoted the two main lines to serve the Irish packet stations. The London & Birmingham Railway, later to become part of the London & North Western Railway, subscribed to the Chester & Holyhead, while the GWR subscribed to the South Wales Railway. The Chester & Holyhead was absorbed by the LNWR in 1859 and the South Wales Railway by the GWR in 1863.

The South Wales Railway had several important engineering features designed by Brunel, among them the Chepstow Bridge across the Wye and the large timber viaducts at Newport and Landore, the latter a third of a mile in length. The 1,200-foot-long viaduct across the Usk at Newport was almost finished when it caught fire on 31 May 1848 and was entirely destroyed. When it was rebuilt, wrought-iron girders were used for the central span. Chepstow to Swansea was opened 18 June 1850. The line was worked by the Great Western Railway, locomotives and rolling stock being ferried across from Bristol.

The line between Gloucester and the east bank of the Wye at Chepstow was opened on 19 September 1851, passengers being conveyed between the two stations across the road bridge. The railway bridge was particularly interesting as the bank was a cliff on one side, and a low bank on the other.

This 300-foot-long span across the Wye consisted of girders supported by suspension chains hung from a horizontal 9-foot-diameter circular tube resting on piers approximately 50 feet above rail level. The tubes, very slightly arched to improved their appearance and to cope better with stresses, prevented the chains dragging the piers inwards. Before the line opened, the journey from London to Swansea, partly by railway and partly by coach, took fifteen hours; it took only five hours when a single-span bridge was opened in July 1852. A second span opened the following April. The line was subsequently extended to Neyland, where passengers were ferried to Pembroke Dock, in 1856.

There were two main links to the West of England: the Great Western and the London & South Western. The former received its Act in 1835. The use of 'Great' in the title was brilliant as it gave confidence to investors, passengers and those seeking carriage of goods. Quite a few other railways eventually adopted the word in their titles: Great Central, Great Northern, Great North of England and Great North of Scotland.

The post of engineer was given to the twenty-seven-year-old Isambard Kingdom Brunel, well known in Bristol for his improvements to the harbour and having submitted designs for the Clifton Suspension Bridge. His concept of a railway was a straight, level line. This was achievable from London to Swindon, but his answer to the falling gradient required westwards was two gradients of 1 in 100 worked by stationary steam power. In the event, in the interim between the line's planning and opening, locomotives had been improved to such an extent that they proved capable of climbing such a gradient.

Not all were in favour of the line – for instance, Eton College was against it as the school practised giving as much freedom to the boys as possible and feared that a railway would encourage them to go to London. The GWR evaded the restriction of not being permitted to construct a station within three miles of the school by the simple expedient of merely stopping trains at Slough and selling tickets at the Crown Inn. Not long after, the college chartered a special train to convey its pupils to London for Queen Victoria's Coronation.

Construction was relatively easy as far as Corsham, but then came Box Tunnel, 3,212 yards in length, followed by eight tunnels between Bath and Bristol, as well as lofty embankments and lengthy viaducts.

Although the standard gauge of 4 feet 8½ inches was generally specified in Acts of Parliament, Brunel persuaded the chairman of the House of Lords Committee to omit the gauge clause as a wider gauge might be of greater public advantage. Brunel said that the larger the wheel, the less friction on the axle, and if the gauge was wider than standard then wheels could be placed outside the centre of gravity, making a much safer method of transport. The gauge of 7 feet was accepted by the GWR directors in 1835.

In 1845, the Gauge Commission considered the benefits of broad and standard gauge and Brunel suggested comparative tests with engines and trains of comparable weight. *Ixion*, a 2-2-2 7-foot single express engine, and *Hercules*, a goods 0-6-0, ran between Paddington and Didcot. *Ixion* averaged 50 mph, with a maximum of 60 mph. On one trip, the train, having been left at Paddington overnight, was found on inspection the next morning to have had the grease in its axle boxes replaced with sand. In their report, the commissioners wrote that 'the Broad Gauge Engines possess greater capabilities for speed with equal loads, and, generally speaking, of propelling greater loads with equal speed; and, moreover, that working with such engines is economical where very high speeds are required, or where the loads to be conveyed are such as to require the full power of the engine'. Although the broad gauge proved superior, the commission favoured the standard gauge as 87.4 per cent of the country's railways were laid to this gauge.

The line between London and Bristol was opened in stages. Reading station was the first of Brunel's one-sided stations, erected in situations where the town was on just one side of the railway. Logically, the Up station was at the Up end and the Down at the other end. This layout had the advantage that passengers and luggage did not have to cross the rails and non-stop trains could run clear of the platforms. In due course, similar stations were erected at Taunton, Exeter and Gloucester. The last section of line, that between Chippenham and Bath, was opened 30 June 1841.

Meanwhile, other railways were planned to extend from the Great Western. The Cheltenham & Great Western Union was planned from Swindon to Gloucester and Cheltenham, while others took the line onwards from Bristol to Penzance – the Bristol & Exeter, the South Devon and the Cornwall Railway. As the latter two railways had steep gradients, tank engines were employed so that all the adhesive weight was placed on the driving wheels and there was less chance of slipping. The Cornwall Railway was impecunious and never paid a dividend;

part of the trouble was the maintenance cost of its many timber viaducts.

Motive power on the South Devon was one of Brunel's serious errors of judgement. In 1839, Joseph Samuda and Samuel Clegg patented an atmospheric railway. An iron pipe was laid between the rails. Along the pipe's top was a slot closed by a leather flap. Into this pipe a piston slung under a special carriage was fitted, and when air was drawn from ahead of the piston by means of stationary engines set at approximate 3-mile intervals along the line, atmospheric pressure from behind would propel the special carriage and likewise the train to which it was attached. Robert Stephenson was not enamoured with the idea, and called it 'a rope of air'.

This novelty appealed to Brunel, and atmospheric traction began on 13 September 1847. The highest speed recorded for an atmospheric train was 68 mph with a train of 28 tons, and an average speed of 35 mph was achieved over 4 miles with a load of 100 tons. After eight months, the system proved a failure. The leather seal was difficult to keep supple as the natural oil was sucked out by the pipe's inlet and outlet valves, while rats enjoyed eating the fat applied to keep the leather soft. Atmospheric working cost 3s 1d per mile compared with just 1s 4d for steam.

By 1850, the Great Western's temporary London station at Bishop's Road was proving inadequate, so early the following year the directors proposed the construction of a new terminus east of Bishop's Road Bridge. It was designed and constructed under Brunel's supervision and with the assistance of Matthew Digby Wyatt. Spacious, it had three departure platforms and two arrivals, with five carriage-storage sidings between; in later years these sidings proved invaluable for offering space for further platforms to be laid.

The other line to the west was that made by the London & South Western. It started off as the London & Southampton, which opened 11 May 1840.

The Dover to Calais packet was reached from London by the South Eastern Railway. It was not allowed a London terminus as Parliament did not desire too many termini in London. The South Eastern was therefore obliged to use the London Bridge terminus of the London & Brighton Railway and its line to Redhill, from where the South Eastern ran a line almost dead straight for 45 miles to Ashford, reaching the coast at Folkestone in 1843. Between Folkestone and Dover, tunnels were driven through the chalk about 150 yards from the cliff face. In February 1844, the first train reached Dover. Using a shorter route, the Chatham line reached Dover in 1861.

Behind the Dover project was the idea of a Channel tunnel that would bring Continental trains to London Bridge. The South Eastern actually sank experimental shafts between Folkestone and Dover (and in doing so found coal), but there was deep suspicion of a tunnel or bridge from France, which would threaten Britain's fortress with invasion; grandparents could still remember Bonaparte's army at Boulogne massed for invasion.

From Corbett's Lane near New Cross to London Bridge, the line was used by three railways: the London & Greenwich, the London & Brighton and the South Eastern. As the points at Corbett's Lane were worked by hand, the world's first railway signal box was opened there. Whether it made travel safer is debatable: a white light indicated 'Clear' to Greenwich trains, while red indicated 'Clear' to the others!

As East Anglia had no coal deposits or large industries, initially there was no demand for railways. In 1836, the Eastern Counties Railway was authorised to build a

London–Colchester–Ipswich–Great Yarmouth line. It decided on a gauge of 5 feet, and in 1839 opened from a temporary terminus at Bethnal Green to Romford. It reached Colchester in 1843, and there it stuck and changed to standard gauge in 1844. The remainder of the line to Great Yarmouth was constructed by three other companies. The last stagecoach left London (for Newmarket and Norwich) in 1846.

The railway bringing to an end the stagecoach industry had an impact on many people. Inns which relied on income from coach passengers were forced to find other income; horse breeders were affected, as were saddlers, farriers, coachbuilders and farmers growing oats for horse feed.

Many canals were bought by the railways, sometimes as the price of being allowed to lay a competitive line, while other canals prospered up to the First World War as they could carry cheap and bulky goods economically when speed was unimportant. However, by 1867 railways had overtaken the canals as principal freight carriers.

It is difficult to fully appreciate the sudden change railways brought to Britain: in 1835, the only significant lines were those around Glasgow and Durham, the Liverpool & Manchester and the Leeds & Selby; yet by 1845, lines radiated from London to Dover, Brighton, Southampton, Exeter, Bristol, Liverpool, Lancaster, Manchester, Hull, Newcastle and Norwich, while in Scotland they ran from Edinburgh to Glasgow and Ayr. The era of the canal and stagecoach had certainly entered its twilight years.

Although most railway promoters were honest and straightforward, a few rogues arose, particularly George Hudson, chairman of the York & North Midland Railway. The company appeared to be extremely prosperous, and in 1844 he gathered other lines to form the Midland Railway with a capital of £5 million. This earned him the title of Railway King. When he resigned the chairmanship of the Eastern Counties Railway in 1849, it came to light that over £200,000 in dividends had been paid out of capital, not profits. Investigation on other railways of which he was chairman revealed similar misappropriation, and he was forced to resign from them all and live abroad in obscurity.

Hudson was not the only one to suffer, as his downfall shook public faith in railway investment. Thousands of people who had purchased railway shares in the hope of a quick profit tried to sell, but the bottom had fallen out of the market. As no one wanted to buy, they discovered that their shares were not worth the paper they were printed on and that their savings had evaporated.

Skilled railwaymen commanded high wages: in the 1840s, a driver could earn between 5s 6d and 7s 6d a day, and firemen between 3s 6d and 5s 6d depending on their length of service. Signalmen earned about £1 2s 0d weekly, while even porters, at 18s 7d a week, were far better off than agricultural labourers at 11s 6d in the North or 8s 5d in the South.

Railwaymen were sometimes required to work overlong hours. M. T. Bass, brewer and MP for Derby, spoke for the men and revealed that train crews were sometimes required to be on duty for nineteen and a half hours and that one driver was on his engine for twenty-nine and a half hours. The *Daily Telegraph* of 26 December 1871 stated that a Nine Elms driver had completed 654 hours' work in the previous six weeks. One guard went to work at 6.35 p.m. on 23 December 1870 and ended his duty at 2.00 p.m. on 25 December. On Christmas Eve he was found asleep in his brake van and, there being no relief guard available, a porter was sent along to 'cheer him up' and 'nudge' him when he 'dropped off'. Captain Tyler of the Board of Trade revealed that an alarming rise in the accident rate was caused by signalmen at work for up to thirty-seven hours.

A Factory Act had been passed limiting the hours of textile workers to twelve hours a day as early as 1833, and further legislation had reduced it to ten by 1850, but, because of the powerful influence of the railway interest in Parliament, the Board of Trade abstained from interfering with the conditions of employment on railways.

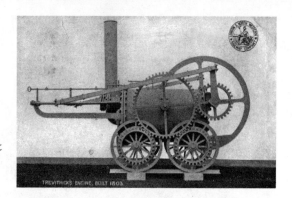

1. Richard Trevithick's locomotive of 1803, depicted on a London & North Western Railway (LNWR) postcard. (Author's collection)

2. An LNWR postcard showing a train of first-class coaches in 1837. At the rear can be seen a Royal Mail van and passengers travelling in their own open carriage placed on a flat wagon. It is to be hoped that it is placed sufficiently far in the rear to prevent smuts getting in their eyes. The picture below depicts second-class passengers, who enjoy a roof and plenty of fresh air. The reader would probably prefer to travel in the coaches of the bottom picture, which shows an LNSWR Anglo-American boat express of 1904. (Author's collection)

3. The 2-2-0 built in 1835 for the Liverpool & Manchester Railway was the first engine to have inside cylinders. (Author's collection)

4. A locomotive built by George Stephenson around 1830 seen still at work on the Hetton colliery railway in July 1901. Note the wooden brake blocks on the front wheels. (Author's collection)

5. A replica of Stephenson's *Rocket* at work in Hyde Park, 27 August 1979. (Revd Alan Newman)

6. The Liverpool & Manchester Railway 0-4-2 *Lion*, built in 1838, seen here at Monkton Combe on 5 July 1952 when used in the film *The Titfield Thunderbolt*. As no provision was made for a bracket, the lamp was hung on the coupling hook. (R. E. Toop)

7. GWR express 4-2-4T No. 2002, built by the Bristol & Exeter Railway as No. 40 in 1873. Withdrawn in 1890, it had 8-foot-10-inch-diameter driving wheels and wooden brake blocks on the bogie wheels. (Author's collection)

8. GWR Hawthorn class 0-6-0 *Hedley*, built in 1865 and fitted with a saddle tank in 1877. Although withdrawn in May 1892 it was not scrapped, instead being used as a quarry stone crusher and in 1905 becoming a stationary boiler at Neath Engineering Department. Its boiler was condemned in 1914, but remained at Neath until sent to Swindon, where it is seen here before cutting up in the summer of 1929, the last surviving broad gauge main-line locomotive. (Author's collection)

9. Comparison of broad and standard gauge locomotives, both named *Rover*. The broad gauge engine on the left was built in 1871 and withdrawn in May 1892. On the right, No. 3019 required its boiler to be raised higher that on its broad gauge predecessor in order to clear the 7-foot-8½-inch-diameter driving wheels. Built as a 2-2-2, it became a 4-2-2 in 1894 and was withdrawn in 1908. (Author's collection)

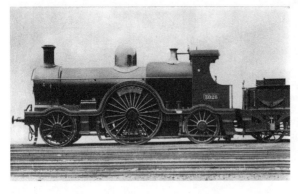

10. No. 3028 was built as a 2-2-2 broad gauge convertible in 1891, altered to standard gauge in August 1892, rebuilt as a 4-2-2 in July 1894 and withdrawn in February 1909. (Author's collection)

11. A stagecoach adapted to run on the Stockton & Darlington Railway. (Author's collection)

12. Saltash Bridge in August/September 1858, with the western span in position and the eastern in the course of being raised. (Author's collection)

13. Mr and Mrs Gladstone experience a ride in a contractor's wagon on the unfinished Metropolitan Railway at Edgware Road, 22 May 1862. (Author's collection)

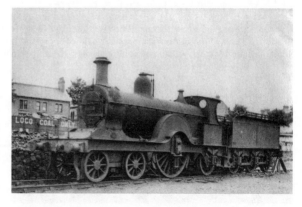

14. Midland Railway 4-2-2 No. 663, built in 1893 and withdrawn in 1926. The invention of steam sanding saw a brief resurgence of single-driver engines in the 1890s. It stands beside a stack of locomotive coal. (Author's collection)

15. The tender of the engine involved in the Tay Bridge disaster of 28 December 1879. (Author's collection)

Sent to the Chicago Exhibition in 1893 where it gained the gold medal for excellence of workmanship and subsequently ran a L. & N.W. train from Chicago to New York, the only British train ever run in America. Specially painted white and with the Royal Arms in honor of Queen Victoria's Diamond Jubilee in 1897.

COMPOUND PASSENGER ENGINE "QUEEN EMPRESS"

16. LNWR compound 2-2-2-2 No. 2054 *Queen Empress*. The text reads, 'Sent to the Chicago Exhibition in 1893 where it gained the gold medal for excellence of workmanship and subsequently ran a L&NW train from Chicago to New York, the only British train ever to run in America. Specially painted white and with the Royal Arms in honor of Queen Victoria's Diamond Jubilee in 1897.' (Author's collection)

17. LNWR compound 2-2-2-2T No. 2000, shown at the Manchester Exhibition in 1887. (Author's collection)

PICKING UP WATER AT FULL SPEED.

18. An LNWR engine at full speed picks up water from troughs. (Author's collection)

19. Midland Railway 0-6-0 No. 3044. Built in 1880, it enjoyed a long life and was not withdrawn until 1958. Note the tender cab to make tender-first working more tolerable. (Author's collection)

M. R. Goods Train With American Engine

20. In 1899, British locomotive builders had full order books. The Midland Railway surmounted the problem by ordering from the USA. This engine, one of ten built by Schenectady, was withdrawn in 1914. (Author's collection)

21. Messrs Baldwin of Philadelphia constructed ten similar engines, but all were withdrawn by 1913, No. 2505 being withdrawn in February 1910. The photograph was taken before 1907, when it was renumbered 2204. (Author's collection)

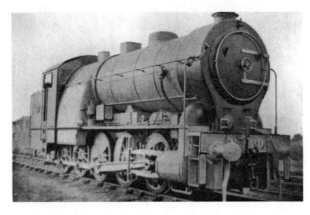

22. The Great Eastern Railway 0-10-0T No. 20, designed to show that a steam-hauled train could accelerate as fast as an electric train. (Author's collection)

23. The driver of LNWR 4-6-0 No. 2445 holds an oil can. Notice the wheel wedges to prevent the locomotive moving. (Author's collection)

24. Great Central Railway 4-6-0 No. 1069. (Author's collection)

25. The huge Glasgow & South Western Railway 4-6-4T No. 2101, used on important suburban services. Note the splashers over its bogies. (Author's collection)

26. An ex-Glasgow & South Western Railway 4-4-0 as LMS No. 14258. It stands on a turntable. (Author's collection)

27. An inside-cylinder ex-Caledonian Railway 4-6-0 as LMS No. 14605. Taken in the mid-1930s, it bears the shed plate 29B, Aberdeen. It stands at a gas-lit coal stage. (Author's collection)

28. The Midland Railway, and also the LMS in its early days, held a short-train-and-small-engine policy, using two engines on heavier trains. Here, 4-4-0 compounds Nos 1129 and 1130 are seen at Coventry around 1928. (Author's collection)

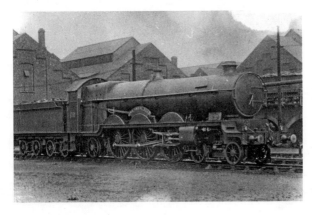

29. 4-6-2 No. 111 *The Great Bear*; note its eight-wheel tender. Locomotive coal wagons stand to the right on a viaduct giving access to a coal stage. (Author's collection)

30. From 1914, railway factories turned to war work in addition to keeping stock in repair. Here, on 25 October 1916, 6 inch naval guns and limbers are on wagons outside the factory at Swindon. (Author's collection)

31. The First World War, left to right: a Midland Railway wagon; a bolster wagon; LNWR bolster wagon, the latter both dumb-buffered. Dumb-buffered wagons were prohibited from running over the main lines from 31 December 1914. (Author's collection)

32. Ex-Caledonian Railway 0-4-4T LMS No. 15134 has a massive coal bunker. (Author's collection)

33. 'Big Bertha' 0-10-0 No. 2290 was built in 1919 for banking trains up the steep Lickey Incline south of Birmingham. As it spent half its life in reverse, the tender cab was essential, as was the headlight in front of the chimney to assist buffering up at night. (Author's collection)

34. A GWR high-sided wagon converted for use by military horses. (Author's collection)

**LANCASHIRE & YORKSHIRE RLY**
**THIRD     CLASS**
**LIVERPOOL (EX) A**
To
**SANDHILLS**
Available on day of issue only
131
TURN OVER}     Sandhills     Fare 1½d

26 JE 91     1601

**G.     R.**
Series 8     Series 8

**FARRINGDON ST** to
FARRINGDON ST.     FARRINGDON ST.
**FINSBURY PARK**
FINSBURY PARK     FINSBURY PARK
Fare 3½d. Third Class Fare 3½d.
SEE CONDITIONS ON BACK.

2412     2412

LANC & YORK. RLY.
Available on
day of issue only.

THIRD CLASS
Southport
TO
EDGE HILL
Via Bootle

ill     Fare 2s3d.

3139

# 5

# Early Rolling Stock and How It Developed; How the Railway Affected Life in Britain

When something new is made, to give confidence to users, it is often designed to look similar to the familiar. Early railway coaches were, therefore, made to look like several stagecoaches joined together and were named like their road predecessors, such as *The Times*, *Victory* and *Wellington*. Many of these vehicles were supplied by workshops that built road vehicles, one example being Joseph Wright, originally an operator of stagecoaches, who founded the Metropolitan Company, later the Metropolitan Railway Carriage & Wagon Co., at Saltley.

Coaches were formed of a wooden body mounted on a wooden underframe with iron or steel running and drawgear. The body framework was often of oak or teak with oak, or teak roof boards covered in canvas. The paint was covered with several coats of protective varnish.

The early stagecoach-like vehicles were for first-class passengers, as the third class, being equivalent to those who travelled on the outside of a stagecoach, were still able to enjoy fresh air by travelling in open wagons often made more luxurious by the addition of benches, while holes in the floor allowed rainwater to drain out to avoid passengers sitting in a puddle, though unfortunately a draught penetrated these holes. The rather more affluent third-class passengers, and those of the second class with open windows, sometimes invested in gauze goggles to guard their eyes from smuts. Some passengers preferred to travel in the familiarity of their horse-drawn coach placed on a flat wagon.

Some railways used Stanhopes for their third-class passengers. These vehicles took the name of the light, open road vehicles called after the Honourable and Reverend Fitzroy Stanhope, for whom they were first made. As there was no provision for seats in these wagons, the name became appropriately corrupted to 'Stan'ups'. In April 1840, the directors of the Glasgow, Paisley, Kilmarnock & Ayr Railway ruled that their new third-class coaches should in future be made without seats, and that where seats had been installed they should be removed.

Rail travel was safer than road, but when an accident did occur it was more spectacular. Fortunately, the 1840 Railways Regulation Act made fatal accidents reportable to the Board of Trade, which could then identify the cause and suggest safety measures to prevent a repetition.

On 13 March 1841, George Stephenson wrote a letter to the president of the Board of Trade, stating that he was 'quite sure that some interference on the part of the government is much wanted'. He suggested that a Board of Trade committee of railway engineers vetted plans for railway working, along with a speed limit of 40 mph on favourable lines, with a reduction round curves; a uniform system of signalling; self-acting brakes, or, as an interim measure, four brake coaches and two brakesmen for each train; six-wheeled engines and coaches; government-inspected wheels, springs and axles; and government arbitration of disputes between companies.

Under the Railway Regulation Act of 1840, accidents were required to be reported to the Railway Department of the Board of Trade, no less than twenty-five fatal accidents being reported in the first three months.

Many railways only ran third-class coaches in goods trains, and these ran mainly at night. On Christmas Eve 1841, a Down goods from Paddington ran into a landslip at Sonning. The abrupt stop caused the goods wagons to crush the open passenger wagons against the tender; eight of the thirty-eight passengers were killed outright and seventeen seriously injured. The Board of Trade report said,

> The third-class carriages have seats 18 inches high, but the sides and ends are only two feet above the floor, so that a person standing up, either when the train is unexpectedly put in motion or stopped is, if near the side or end, in great danger of being thrown out of the carriage and those sitting near the sides are also in danger of falling; besides which, the exposure to the cutting winds of the winter must be very injurious to the traveller, who, if proceeding from London to Bristol, often remains exposed for ten or twelve hours, a great part of which is in the night-time.

The Board of Trade investigated the conditions of third-class passengers on various railways and the result was Gladstone's Railway Act of 1844, which required a closed third-class coach to be provided on a minimum of one train daily, with that train travelling at not less than 12 mph including stops – this was a faster speed than the stagecoach of a few years before – and at a fare not exceeding a penny per mile. They were known as 'parliamentary trains'. In return for providing parliamentary trains, railway companies were exempt from paying a passenger tax of 5 per cent on fares. Unfortunately, this information about third-class closed coaches was not widely disseminated and on 14 March 1845, John Jonathan, a wire worker aged about fifty, travelled from Bristol to Bath in a third-class open coach – his wife walked as they had insufficient money for two tickets.

After arriving at Bath following the 10-mile journey, Mr Jonathan was frozen stiff and unable to leave his coach unaided. A porter assisted him to the platform and then carried him down the stairs to street level. Here he was placed on the pavement, where he died. Ironically, a closed third-class coach was included in the train, but Mr Jonathan was not aware that he could use it.

Open wagons were still used on cheap excursion trains following the 1844 Act, while on the Sheffield, Ashton & Manchester Railway the first cattle trucks, ordered in 1845, were 'to be fitted with spring buffers and drawbars, to answer occasionally for passengers'.

Around 1850, the London & North Western Railway ran a train of third-class coaches from London to Liverpool starting between six and seven in the morning and arriving at Liverpool, Manchester and Leeds that same evening. It travelled at an average speed of 15 mph. On arrival at Blisworth it was detained for an hour and a half, ostensibly to allow the mail and three other fast trains to overtake, whereas the true reason was to encourage passengers to use first class in order to secure a faster journey. Thirty-minute stops were also provided at Birmingham and Derby. Even this was better than just a few years before, when a third-class passenger took two days to travel from London to Liverpool.

Early first-class coaches were quite sumptuous and generally carried on four wheels. Second-class coaches were often of the same length but had more compartments, thus offering less room. They were roofed, but generally there was no glass in the windows and so passengers were exposed above shoulder height to the elements. The third-class coaches in the later 1840s had sides of solid wood with small Venetian vents, or sliding shutters at the top to give ventilation and enable passengers, when standing, to identify their location. Although seeming primitive to twenty-first-century passengers, this was much more pleasant than travelling on the outside of a stagecoach. The Great Western Railway's cosy third-class coaches seated fifty-nine passengers in a space only 20 feet 9 inches by 8 feet 6 inches, the sixtieth seat occupied by the brakesman. As the door was only 18 inches wide, portly passengers had to enter sideways.

In most of the early coaches, a moderately tall man could not stand up in a railway carriage with his hat on. He could nurse it on his knees if sitting down, or later insert it in a pair of cords stretched on the ceiling above his seat. Heavy luggage was stowed on the roof, while hand luggage was supposed to be placed under the seat opposite that of its owner.

As Hamilton Ellis wrote in *British Railway History 1830–1876*,

One can only imagine the predicament of the shy, polite young man, travelling to Rugby anxious to recover his carpet bag from behind the massive and most virginal petticoats of the lady opposite, who was going through to Birmingham, and who advised him that if he attempted to enter into conversation with her, she would inform the station police.

Sam Fay, superintendent of the London & South Western, revealed in *A Royal Road* that the early first-class coaches had compartments so narrow that travellers' knees were pressed uncomfortably hard against those of their opposite neighbour. Much as a first-class passenger might grumble at the small space allotted him, his fellow traveller in a second class had far greater discomfort to complain of; his seat was a bare board, his knees in as close proximity to his vis-à-vis as in the superior carriage, and unless provided with a good umbrella, the chances argued in favour of a wet skin, for all second-class carriages were open to the weather on either side. First-class luggage was loaded on the roof, while all belongings of second-class passengers were deposited in two boots placed across their carriage, underneath the seats, and opening from the outside.

A frame work with seats, fitted on the bed of a carriage truck, constituted the vehicle in which third-class passengers travelled; the frame work was removed upon the truck being required for its ordinary purpose. On a wet day the condition of the poor wretches condemned by poverty to travel in such conveyances may be more easily imagined than described; if they turned their backs to the storm the rain ran down their necks, if they faced it their eyes became blinded and their pockets filled with water; an umbrella was a useless impediment, and their truck really resolved itself into a species of horizontal shower bath from whose searching power there was no escape.

The Liverpool & Manchester Railway used the word 'class' to describe *trains*, a 'first-class' train being the fastest, but the Grand Junction Railway referred to first-class or second-class *passengers*. Until then, first and second class had only been used as a term for performance in university examinations. Railways seemed obsessed with class: first- and second-class passengers used separate booking offices and waiting rooms, while third-class passengers used goods stations, but this was for the practical reason that the latter travelled by goods train. Basically, first-class passengers enjoyed well-padded seats, second-class seats were thinly padded, while third-class seats were merely boards. In 1845, the Edinburgh & Glasgow Railway provided a fourth class in addition to the parliamentary one. The first company never to offer second class was the Great North of Scotland, which opened in 1854.

Naturally, first-class passengers, paying a higher fare, won the benefit of each advancement in passenger comfort: sleeping cars on the London & Birmingham in 1838, foot warmers on the Great Western in 1856, Pullman cars with steam heating on the Midland in 1874, dining cars on the Great Northern in 1879, gas lighting on the Metropolitan and Great Eastern between 1876 and 1878, electric lighting on the London, Brighton & South Coast in 1881 and corridor coaches and lavatories on the Great Eastern and Great Western in 1891. All these luxuries eventually filtered down to the second and third classes.

Until the provision of toilets, the wise placed a pot in their luggage, the contents of which were tipped out of the window – or sometimes there was the rash and dangerous opening of a door. Gentlemen had the alternative, instead of using a pot, of wearing a rubber tube fixed down the trouser leg to end in a suitable container. There was no such comparable invention for ladies.

# Lighting

Each early first-class compartment usually had a rape-oil lamp to itself, whereas those in third class, if they had a light at all, had to share, sometimes just one to a whole coach. The Great

Western provided no coach lighting until 1842. As time went on and improvements were demanded, two second- or third-class compartments shared a lamp which was placed centrally above the partition, a section by the lamp being cut out to allow light to enter both compartments.

Oil lamps were smoky and the oil often oozed out, filling the glass globe with a dirty, dark-coloured liquid which impeded light, making reading almost impossible. Lamp men at the larger stations earned a tip by installing a newly trimmed lamp into a compartment where passengers were eager to read. Delinquent boys thought it fun to try and head a lamp out of its hole.

To guard against fire risk, a lamp room was usually placed in a remote part of the station. Iron-framed tables with slate tops were set up in these rooms. A lamp was placed into a hole in a bench so it could be easily held without slipping when rubbed and scrubbed. The lamp cisterns held about a pint of oil, sufficient to burn for twenty-four hours. When a train required lamping, lamp barrows were wheeled along the platform. If the lamps already on the train were unused, the lamp man on the roof lit them with a torch. If there were no lamps, or they were dirty and needed changing, then fresh lamps were hauled up on a hooked pole, while the used lamps were dexterously dropped into the hands of a lamp man on the platform. The lamps weighed between 15 and 18 lb each.

In the late 1850s, the next improvement was to adopt gas lighting. A few companies, such as the Lancashire & Yorkshire and the North London Railway, used coal gas, but most preferred oil gas obtained from shale oil. The oil was fed by gravitation to a red-hot retort, where it was vaporised, condensed to a gas holder and stored at a pressure of 150 lb/sq. inch. Pipes conveyed it to the carriage sidings. As required, it was fed into a reservoir, a cylinder of rubber and canvas below the coach and built to withstand pressure of 150 lb, though in practice it was only filled to 110 lb. Each coach had two cylinders measuring 7 feet by 1 feet 1 inches, and these would store sufficient gas for twenty lights burning for twenty to twenty-four hours. The Great Western used Scottish paraffin shale, which it found preferable to the Russian or American oils. Travelling gas tanks carried supplies to places without an oil-gas works. Gas lighting assisted ventilation as oxygen was obtained from inside the coach and replaced by fresh air from outside. Initially the problem of gas mantles was not solved, as shock and vibration damaged the incandescent mantles, and so fishtail burners lasted longer on railways than they did in the home.

From the first, the Great Western's carriages on the broad gauge were far superior to those found on other companies' lines. Third-class traffic was sparse as nobody used it unless unavoidable. In the returns made to the Gauge Commissioners in 1845, the Great Western had 106 first-class carriages, 103 second-class and only eight third-class.

One writer, describing an early trip on the Liverpool & Manchester, said, 'I cannot say that I at all liked it; the speed was too great to be pleasant, and certainly it is not smoother and easier than a turnpike road. When the carriages stop and go on, a very violent jolting takes place, from the ends of the carriage jostling together.'

A great improvement in comfort came in the early 1830s when Henry Booth, a Liverpool corn merchant who became a director of the London & North Western Railway, invented the screw coupling, enabling buffers to be drawn together and thus avoiding most of the bumps and jerks each time a train stopped or started. Early coaches had their solebars extended and padded with leather or horsehair to form buffers, but before 1835 spring buffers were used.

Shortly after the opening of the Liverpool & Manchester Railway, Colonel Pownall Phipps of the East India Company wrote that the coaches had

three bodies holding six persons each; the seats being divided by small bars. They are regularly numbered, and the ticket delivered at the office shows the seat to which you are entitled.

We first passed on the road a string of carriages like our own, coming from Liverpool. The velocity with which both bodies are moving, separated only by a space of two or three feet, gave a terrific appearance to this occurrence, although, in reality, there is no danger, when each person keeps his seat, and does not put the head out of the window. We next passed, in the same manner, some open cars, the price of a seat in which is only two shillings and six pence; but passengers are exposed to inconvenience from the steam and in winter they must be very cold, going so rapidly through the air. The last carriages we passed were platforms laden with merchandise and poultry. A gentleman's carriage was conveyed on one of these platforms.

On arrival at a tunnel near Liverpool the steam-carriage [engine] was taken off, and the coaches slowly moved under the rocky arch by ropes turned by steam, and on clearing the dark passage, omnibuses were in readiness to convey passengers to their inns. Two hundred tons of cotton had recently been conveyed in one trip by two locomotive engines, in two hours and a half, the charge for which was one hundred pounds, or about a farthing for conveying four pounds and a half of cotton thirty-one miles.

The murder of Thomas Briggs in a compartment of a North London Railway train by Franz Muller in 1864 led, for a time, to the provision of Muller's lights. These were openings in compartment partitions that enabled nearby passengers to observe any misdemeanours, but were also of great value to peeping toms.

E. L. Ahrons, in *Locomotive and Train Working in the Latter Part of the Nineteenth Century*, reveals that some of the South Eastern passenger stock was primitive even in the 1880s. Coaches, he says,

> took the form of a cheerless bare rectangular box with hard wooden seats and 'half-way' partitions separating the compartments. The partitions were so low that when the passenger sat down with his back to one of them, his head nearly collided with the back hair and best hat of the female in the next compartment. The carriage floor was constructed on the atmospheric principle, and when the train was moving a violent gale frequently raged in those latitudes which lay below the seats. There were usually two oil lamps of about half candle-power to each carriage, and as there were four compartments, the allowance of light was 0.5 lamp per compartment. The centre of each lamp was above one of the backboards or partitions.
>
> The interior of a first-class carriage was, of course, quite comfortable, for the first-class passenger on the Southern lines was in those days considered to be a person of exceptional quality. Moreover, the first-class fare for any distance above 20 miles was considerably more than most of the carriages were individually worth. The fare from London to Dover, for instance, was estimated by competent statistical authorities who used this railway to be approximately equal to the value of four complete South Eastern coaches of average quality.

The one good thing about South Eastern coaches was that they used solid Mansell wheels with wood centres, invented on that railway and eventually adopted by most British companies. Richard C. Mansell, carriage superintendent for 1848–82, constructed from an iron or steel boss, a disc built from sixteen teak segments. First patented in 1848, by 1874 some 20,000 sets were in use on various British railways and no failure had been reported to the Board of Trade. Mansell wheels stopped being supplied to new stock from just prior to 1914.

Railway sleeping arrangements were initially primitive, being merely twin sticks and a cushion hired from the guard, placed across the foot space of an ordinary compartment. The very first British sleeping car was produced by the North British in 1873.

The practice of slipping coaches from moving trains went back to at least 1843, when the Hayle Railway in Cornwall slipped passenger coaches from the rear of mineral wagons when approaching Hayle. The locomotive and wagons carried on to North Quay, taking with them the guard who had made the slip by lifting a coupling. While the carriages were still in motion, horses were hitched on to draw them into the passenger station. It was fraught with risks and one day when the mineral train became derailed it was struck by the coaches it had just slipped.

Slipping at intermediate stations first occurred in February 1858 when the London, Brighton & South Coast's Down express running non-stop East Croydon to Brighton slipped coaches for Lewes and Hastings at Haywards Heath.

# Goods Stock

Until the end of the twentieth century, there was hardly any evolution in railway goods vehicles. There were two types of four-wheeled wagons, both constructed of wood: the chaldron, which carried one imperial chaldron, or 2 tons 13 cwt of coal; and the flat truck. The upper part of the sides of a chaldron tapered outwards and solebar extensions produced wooden dumb buffers. Flat trucks were for carrying anything which could be secured by being lashed under tarpaulins. A third variety of wagon soon appeared, an open wagon with straight sides and ends with semi-circular tops to support a sheet without ripping it. The Great Western favoured six-wheeled open wagons, many built of iron instead of timber. Having twice the capacity of a four-wheeler, they only cost about a third as much again to build. Some railways owned no wagons at all, those used being the property of private owners.

By the mid-nineteenth century, other wagons had been designed. These included the box van, for carrying merchandise which could not be exposed to the weather; a flat timber wagon with iron stanchions to hold the load; cattle wagons; ballast wagons; and vans for gunpowder and corpses. The Great Western had some unusual horseboxes, wider than they were long, so one can imagine that the horses enjoyed an excitable ride.

Larger wagons were more economical to haul as they had less dead weight, and, in 1888, J. L. Wilkinson, the Great Western's chief goods manager, persuaded his directors to build a 25-ton open wagon carried on bogies. Unfortunately, it proved impossible to receive a satisfactory load to fill it and make it an economic proposition, so the use of the standard 10-ton wagon continued. In some cases, larger wagons were incapable of entering sharply curved private sidings of many factories, mines and quarries.

Towards the end of the nineteenth century passenger trains had continuous brakes, but for freight trains the only brakes were on the engine, tender and brake van. Each wagon had a brake which could be applied by hand when shunting, or applied when a train was stationary at the head of a gradient, but there was no continuous brake available when a train was running. As there was always the danger of a coupling breaking and wagons running away down an incline, a catch point was installed at its foot to derail a runaway.

Wagons normally only had the brake handle on one side. This made it very dangerous for shunters, who frequently had to cross a line to apply the brake. To avoid such fatalities, the Railway Clearing House insisted in due course that all new wagons were required to have brakes on both sides. Dumb buffers were phased out 1 December 1914, and springless buffers only permitted for used within industrial lines.

In 1903, the Great Western equipped some wagons with continuous brakes, which enabled them to run express freights. This move was adopted by other railways, but unbraked goods trains remained the norm until the 1960s. Slow, unbraked goods trains caused a problem when the speed of passenger trains increased as they could take a long time to pass through a section. The problem was solved in some places by running goods trains at night, or quadrupling the tracks.

Heavier trains demanded more powerful engines, but, as their size was constrained by the loading gauge, locomotive efficiency was improved by such measures as superheating, compounding and heated feed water. The weight of an engine rose from 30–40 tons to 100 tons or more. This additional weight demanded heavier permanent way and stronger bridges.

In the event of emergency it was really necessary for there to be some means of communication between the guard and a driver, but it took fifty years before a satisfactory solution was found.

In 1847, the GWR built a rearwards-facing hooded seat on the back of its tender so that the travelling porter could cast his eye along the train and advise the driver if anything was amiss; critics of this railway referred to him as 'the man in the iron coffin'. In 1853, the London & South Western had a device whereby the guard could sound a distinctive tone whistle on the engine to attract his attention, while the driver could blow a shrill whistle to ask him to apply the brakes. On some other lines a cord was suspended under the eaves of passenger coaches, but this had limited use as there was always a considerable amount of slack to draw in before it sounded a warning gong on the tender. Then, by the time the correct tension had been achieved, it may have been too late for the warning to be of use.

By 1877, electric bells had been adopted by the London & South Western, the London, Brighton & South Coast and the South Eastern Railways, but this system was not taken up by the other companies because it was not infallible. When W. H. Preece, London & South Western telegraph superintendent, demonstrated it to the Institution of Civil Engineers, it failed due to dust pollution. A member of the audience remarked that if there was enough dust in the lecture theatre to cause a problem, there would be more than enough on the railway!

As a consequence of the Regulation of Railways Act of 1889 requiring all passenger trains to have continuous brakes, the Manchester, Sheffield & Lincolnshire and the London, Brighton & South Coast adopted chains or handles by which passengers could apply the continuous brakes, though for safety the driver still had a certain amount of control so that the train would not be halted in a tunnel or on a bridge.

From the mid-1840s, it was realised that some form of continuous brake which could be operated from the locomotive was required for passenger trains. A popular mechanical system was the Clark chain brake, whereby a friction clutch on one axle of a brake van operated a windlass to tighten the chain which applied the brakes on adjoining vehicles. The Highland and Lancashire & Yorkshire companies used Newall's and Fay's mechanical continuous brakes, worked by a revolving shaft throughout the train, with universal joint couplings between the carriages.

It was then realised that brakes could be operated by air: either atmospheric pressure operating against a partial vacuum, or compressed air being used to apply the brakes. Vacuum brakes were of two types: simple and automatic.

The simple vacuum system was the cheapest and was developed in the United States by James Young Smith. To apply the brakes, an ejector on the engine exhausted a pipe running throughout the train and this applied the brakes. Although reliable, its failing was that, in the event of a train being divided, the sections would not have their brakes automatically applied.

A better but more expensive system was the automatic vacuum. Designed by James Gresham, the ejector was on continuously, the vacuum holding the brakes off. To apply the brakes the vacuum was destroyed; thus it was fail-safe, for the brakes on all the vehicles would automatically be applied if a train divided.

In the United States, George Westinghouse produced the air brake in 1869. Initially only a simple brake, following a trial on the London, Brighton & South Coast Railway in 1875 he developed an automatic version. Although quick acting, it had the disadvantage that it was not possible to ease the brake off if a train was about to stop short, having to be fully released and then reapplied. The Brighton company was one of the first British companies to adopt an efficient brake and thus pay due regard to the safety of its passengers. By June 1879, fifty-four of its engines and 513 carriages had been fitted with the Westinghouse brake.

In 1874, Colonel Hutchinson of the Board of Trade told the Royal Commission on Railway Accidents that of the eighty-five accidents he had investigated in 1873, thirty five would have been prevented or mitigated by continuous brakes in the hands of the drivers.

In 1875, the Royal Commission on Railway Accidents held brake trials at Newark. The commissioners concluded that 'a good continuous brake will reduce the stopping distances of fast trains to one-third of the distance by which they can be stopped by the present ordinary means' and that 'every train should be provided with sufficient brake power to stop it absolutely within 500 yards at the highest speed at which it travels and upon any gradient upon the line'.

The best systems were Westinghouse and the automatic vacuum. Some companies, such as the Caledonian, Great Eastern, London, Brighton & South Coast and North British, chose the Westinghouse brake, while others settled on the vacuum – some even opted for the simple vacuum, although they changed their views following a series of accidents which could have been avoided had the automatic brake been installed. A fact in favour of the vacuum brake was that the constant air pressure of the Westinghouse brake tended to open the joints and therefore create leakage, whereas with the vacuum brake the pressure from outside helped to close them and thus minimise any defects which could arise.

A collision in Ireland on 12 June 1879 had far-reaching effects in Britain. From Armagh, the line climbed almost continuously at 1 in 75/82 for 3 miles. The single line was not worked on the absolute block system, and passenger trains were despatched at a ten-minute time interval, or twenty minutes for a passenger train following a goods.

Thomas McGrath, the driver, arrived with 2-4-0 No. 86, only a four-coupled engine because his depot at Dundalk was expecting a maximum load of thirteen vehicles – two brake vans and eleven coaches. Arriving at Armagh, he was horrified to find he was expected to haul fifteen vehicles packed with 940 passengers, two-thirds of them children from a Sunday school. He complained to the stationmaster, John Foster, who retorted, 'Any driver who comes here doesn't grumble about taking an excursion train with him.' Thomas replied, 'Why didn't you send proper word to Dundalk? Then I should have had a proper six-coupled engine with me.'

James Elliot, chief clerk, suggested that Patrick Murphy, in charge of the regular train which was to follow the excursion, should supply rear banking assistance to the summit. However, Thomas, nettled by the stationmaster's remark, refused the offer and, at 10.15 a.m., in full forward gear, opened the regulator.

Then, 210 yards from the summit, the engine stalled. Thomas knew that it was useless to attempt a restart: the gauge showed a steam pressure of 125 lb, only 5 lb below the maximum.

Thomas had two choices: he could either wait for Patrick Murphy to arrive with the lightly loaded train and be given a push over the summit, or the train could be divided, the first half being taken to Hamilton's Bawn, the next station, and left there while he returned for the second half. The former course would have been simpler, safer and saved time, but Chief Clerk Elliot, accompanying the train, decided that it should be divided, and Thomas agreed.

It was believed that the siding at Hamilton's Bawn was partly filled with wagons and could only hold five coaches, so the excursion was split between the fifth and sixth coaches.

Unfortunately, the coaches were fitted with the non-automatic vacuum brake, which meant that when the couplings and pipe were disconnected there was no continuous brake.

Elliot ordered Thomas Henry, the rear guard, crammed into his brake compartment with fifteen passengers, to screw his handbrake down hard and then scotch some wheels with stones. Elliot was completely disregarding the rule which stated that 'with a heavy train the guard must not leave his van until perfectly satisfied that his brake will hold the train securely'.

Meanwhile, William Moorhead, the front guard, had placed stones under the wheels of the sixth coach and undid the coupling.

Unfortunately, Thomas McGrath eased back slightly when starting– inevitable due to the delay between releasing the brakes and the time when the pistons drove the train forward. This pushed the ten coaches over the stones, and it all ran back. Guard Thomas Henry jumped back into his van and, with the help of two passengers, tried to get another turn on the handbrake, but it was useless.

The front guard told Thomas McGrath, who attempted to re-couple the two portions. Twice he nearly succeeded but fell over lengths of rail. Unfortunately, in the panic, no one thought of using a piece of rail as a sprag.

To prevent unauthorised entry, all the coach doors had been locked before the train left Armagh, so, except for those in the van with the guard, no one could escape.

Meanwhile, Patrick Murphy had left Armagh with the regular train and, with only a horse box, two vans and three coaches, was romping up the bank at 30 mph. Midway up, his fireman spotted the ten coaches hurtling towards them. At the moment of impact, Murphy had slowed to 5 mph.

The brake van and first two coaches of the excursion were

destroyed, the guard's van fortunately empty as its occupants had jumped out.

Patrick Murphy's engine was bowled off the track by the excursion coaches and his train started to run backwards – first the two coaches and two vans, followed some distance behind by the horsebox and locomotive tender.

The guard stopped his train a quarter of a mile below the site of the collision, but this could have caused a further accident when the horsebox and tender struck it. Fortunately, Patrick Murphy, although dazed, had the wits to screw down the tender brake and stop it and the horsebox three carriages short of the rest of his train.

The catastrophe killed eighty people, twenty-two of them children; a further 262 passengers were injured.

The disaster shocked the public, and before the end of the year a Bill was in Parliament making the provision of continuous automatic brakes and absolute block working compulsory on all British railways.

Safety was greatly improved when the London, Chatham & Dover introduced 'lock and block' in 1882, whereby signals and points were locked to a telegraph instrument, thus preventing a conflicting move being made. It also introduced track circuiting where a train's position was displayed electrically in a signal box.

Boiler explosions were all too common in the early days of railways. Apart from accident, they could be caused by either the boiler becoming weakened, the safety valves failing to release steam, or the collapse of the firebox caused when, due to low water level, heat had softened the metal. In the first two instances the cab may protect the crew from serious harm, but in the last instance the result would probably be fatal.

The very earliest steam engines had boilers made from small iron plates, but by the late 1830s ironmasters were able to roll longer plates so that the first Liverpool & Manchester engines were built of only four plates, each measuring 8 feet by 3 feet.

To prevent steam pressure rising above that for which the boiler was designed, the first safety valves had a weighted lever holding the valve on seating. Until the opening of the Liverpool & Manchester, steam pressure did not usually exceed 50 lb/sq. inch.

As railways grew, so did the steam pressure. The London & North Western Jenny Lind class worked at 120 lb in 1847, and by 1865 that company had engines pressed to 150 lb, while by the end of the century they were 180–200 lb. After Bessemer developed his steelmaking process in 1856, steel began to be used for boiler barrels. A British firebox is generally of copper with a water space of approximately 4 inches between the casing and each of the sides. A working boiler must have water both surrounding the box and several inches deep on the flat top of the firebox.

Initially boilers were filled with water by a hand-operated pump, but soon this tiresome task was obviated by mechanical means, the quantity admitted governed by cocks. The mechanical pump meant that if an engine were stationary for a period, a driver would have to run his engine up and down a siding to top up the boiler. A cunning alternative was to grease the rails, apply the tender handbrake, open the regulator and let the driving wheels slip. The pump problem was overcome by the Frenchman Henri Giffard, who invented the injector in 1859, whereby a jet of steam introduced water into the boiler.

A locomotive normally has two vertical glass-tube water gauges showing the height of water in the boiler itself. They are usually fixed so that when the water is at the bottom of the glass there are still 2–3 inches of water on the firebox crown sheet. A fireman aims to keep the water level about an inch from the top of the gauge; if he allowed it to be higher, his engine could start to prime and water could get into the cylinders.

Due to the motion of a locomotive on the early track, the weights on the safety valves bounced and let more steam escape than was supposed to. A spring-worked valve was found more suited to the purpose. George Salter & Co. patented the spring balance in 1838.

Unfortunately, these early safety valves could be tampered with, and if, say, a train stalled on a steep gradient, it was easier to hang something on the valve to increase boiler pressure than it was to divide the train and take it up in two parts. John Ramsbottom, engineer to the London & North Western in 1856, designed a valve which could not be meddled with yet could be tested to make sure it operated. Another safety device is fusible plugs fitted to the firebox crown. These contain lead so that in the event of the plug not being covered with water, the lead will melt and allow a small jet of steam to enter the firebox and thus give the crew warning. Eugene Bourdon invented the pressure gauge, whereby steam pressure causes a bent tube to open out and in doing so moves a rack which turns a hand to indicate the pressure.

The first boiler explosion occurred on 31 July 1815 at Philadelphia, County Durham, when the boiler of Brunton's *Mechanical Traveller* exploded, killing sixteen and injuring about forty. The Stockton & Darlington saw two explosions in 1828, one on 19 March scalding two firemen, one fatally, while the driver, George Stephenson's older brother, was unhurt. On 1 July, the famous *Locomotion* exploded, killing its driver. Rebuilt, it worked until 1841.

In 1836, the 0-2-2T *Surprise* was tested on the Birmingham

& Gloucester Railway. On 10 November it lived up to its name when its thin boiler plates burst, killing both driver and fireman. This incident was the very first boiler explosion report from a railway company to be received by the Railway Inspectorate.

One dramatic explosion happened on the broad gauge Bristol & Gloucester Railway. A 0-6-0 was hauling a twenty-wagon goods on 8 January 1853, but, when just short of Fishponds, stalled on the 1 in 75 gradient. The driver decided to divide the train, so he and his fireman made their way towards the brake van in order to scotch the wheels of the rear wagons to prevent them from rolling back. The engine had only been standing for a couple of minutes when there was a violent explosion. The boiler had blown up, sending the dome and half the boiler casing over a row of cottages to land a quarter of a mile away. The cause was initially attributed to faulty safety valves set to blow off at 65 lb, but meticulous tests led to the conclusion that the cause was a lack of water in the boiler.

Although mid-Victorian boilers were relatively small, they could do a lot of damage exploding. On 4 July 1861, 2-2-2 No. 249 was hauling the 8.25 p.m. Irish Mail from Euston to Holyhead when, about 4 miles north of Rugby, its boiler burst into several large pieces, many striking bridge piers. The engine's right-hand 7-foot driving wheel was broken off its axle by one piece of boiler. As No. 249 stopped it fell over, derailing all eight passenger coaches. The fireman was killed, but the rest of the train crew escaped serious injury and passengers only suffered 'alarm and severe shocks'. Its boiler was 11¾ feet long and 4 feet in diameter and pressed to only 120 lb, yet gave way to the steam pressure.

The iron plates of boilers were connected by riveted lap joints in the early days, but in 1866, William Kirtley, superintendent of the works at Derby and nephew of Matthew Kirtley, gave a lecture before the Institution of Mechanical Engineers, pointing out the superiority and strength of adopting double-strip butt joints. This avoided grooving occurring along the lap seams, which caused the plates to become thin and unable to withstand the steam pressure. Grooving had caused many boiler explosions in the early 1860s, and probably the one that inspired him to write his report occurred on 5 May 1864. In this instance, 0-6-0 No. 356, built in 1854, was ready to leave Colne when its boiler burst, sixteen large pieces of jagged plate and many other bits flying in all directions. The roof of a house almost 500 yards away was penetrated by a safety valve, which injured an old lady lying in bed. Captain Tyler, in his Board of Trade report, discovered that corrosion had almost eaten entirely through the almost half-inch iron plate. Frighteningly, he wrote that 'of the 6,500 locomotive engines and upwards which are in use on the railways of the United Kingdom, a large proportion are affected by corrosion to an extent which is more or less dangerous'.

It was not always the boiler which caused problems. On 30 November 1878, *Iago*, a broad gauge 0-6-0ST, was due to leave Penzance for Plymouth at 3.50 p.m. when its steam dome blew off. Formed of cast iron and carrying two safety valves, weighty though it was, it soared high into the air, crashed through the station roof and smashed a hole in the roof of an empty carriage standing in a siding and came to rest on the compartment floor. A few days previously, fitters had spotted steam leaking from the dome, half an inch thick and 15 inches in diameter, and renewed the gasket, though a more careful inspection would have revealed a 9-inch-long crack in the dome itself.

Accumulation of scale can cause a firebox to collapse. On 9 April 1906, the Lancashire & Yorkshire 2-4-2T No. 869 was hauling the 9.30 p.m. passenger from Stockport to Colne and had just passed through The Oaks station when its firebox crown sheet burst, scalding the driver while the fireman was injured when he fell from the cab. Scale just under half an inch thick had deprived the crown sheet of water, so it became weakened by the heat of the fire. Although the boiler was supposed to have been washed out every eight days, the accumulation suggested that this had not been done for two or three weeks.

Sometimes a boiler could explode through someone just making a simple mistake. On 21 April 1909, the boiler of Rhymney Railway 0-6-2T No. 97 burst. Why? The previous day a fitter had been dismantling its safety valve and, when reassembling it, made a slight error which made the two safety valves hold hard to their seats by the safety links, instead of being held by the coil spring. Consequently, excessive steam pressure caused the boiler to burst.

Gradients affect water level in a boiler. On 29 April 1912, South Eastern & Chatham Railway 4-4-0 No. 216 was running tender-first with four empty coaches on a rising gradient of 1 in 100. This caused the water to run away from the firebox end and left the level about 4 inches below the crown sheet, causing the firebox roof to collapse. The fireman should have anticipated the gradient and filled the boiler.

The very last big boiler explosion occurred on 11 November 1921 at Buxton, when the boiler of London & North Western compound 0-8-0 No. 134 exploded when its safety valves failed to lift.

In the post-war period, the London & North Western was sending locomotives to engineering firms which had hitherto been busy with war work but were finding it difficult to occupy the employees following the Armistice. In 1920, No. 134 was sent to such a works in Glasgow for overhaul and was returned in July

1921. The valves had been left very tight in the gunmetal bushes. It was an exceptionally cold morning and the low temperature made the fit of the valves tighter and thus prevented the boiler pressure releasing them.

What is surprising is that no guidance was ever given to footplate crews regarding what level of water should be maintained on various gradients; it was only guesswork that told them the depth of water on a locomotive's crown sheet.

The LNER had the excellent system where every water gauge back plate was painted with diagonal black and white lines, so that when seen through a gauge glass these lines appeared to slope the opposite way and thus there was no difficulty in telling at a glance whether the glass was full or empty. Unfortunately, not all companies adopted this practice.

The Lancashire & Yorkshire Railway actually had a locomotive boiler stolen. It happened one Sunday when thieves, hired by an unscrupulous mill owner, broke into the company's works at Miles Platting, Manchester.

Concerned at the expensive of coke, which contemporary locomotives used as smokeless fuel, James Cudworth, locomotive superintendent of the South Eastern, designed a patent firebox to burn coal slack, which was cheaper. His patent firebox had two separate grates, each with a fire door. The grates were fired alternately so that one had a bright fire when fresh coal was burning through on the other. Its disadvantage was that unequal expansion caused trouble to the complicated joints and riveted seams.

Joseph Beattie of the London & South Western came up with a similar idea, but he had a transverse partition in the firebox. There were two fire holes: the lower fed the back chamber and the upper fed the front. The fire in the front chamber was kept in red-hot incandescent condition, while most of the fresh coal was fired into the rear chamber, so that the smoke and unburnt gases passed over the partition into the front chamber, where combustion was completed by the incandescent fuel.

Unfortunately for Beattie and Cudworth, very soon afterwards, in 1858 the Midland Railway invented the brick arch, which did the same job more cheaply and simply and could be used in an ordinary firebox. The deflector plate had also just been introduced on the Birkenhead Railway, and between them the brick arch and deflector plate won, proving a cheaper method of forcing the gases to make a longer journey before reaching the boiler and giving them more time to completely combust.

Boiler pressure was about 120 lb/sq. inch in the mid-nineteenth century, but in the 1870s Francis Webb of the London & North Western Railway started making boilers of steel rather than wrought iron. By 1895, 175 lb boilers were common, while in the mid-twentieth century large locomotives were pressed to 250 lb.

The tenders designed by William Stroudley of the London, Brighton & South Coast were unusual in having inside frames. This was so that their wheels were interchangeable with the carrying wheels of tank and express engines. Stroudley stated that there was therefore no necessity to allow the wheels to remain in the leading end of an engine after the tyres had worn below a certain thickness, 'as they would run with safety in a tender, when it would not be judicious to use them under the engine'.

Another of Stroudley's ideas was to place a large, coupled wheel at the leading end of the engine. In a lecture to the Institution of Civil Engineers in 1885, he explained his reasons for this radical departure:

> By placing the coupled wheels forward, where the greatest weight
> is, the hinder part of the engine may have small wheels, the base

be shortened, and the use of heavy cast-iron weights at the back of the engine dispensed with. It is found that an engine runs much more smoothly when the centre of gravity is kept well forward. The large leading wheels pass over the points, crossings, etc., very easily; causing less disturbance than small ones. They pass round curves without shock or oscillation, which is no doubt owing to the small weight upon the trailing wheels, as it is the trailing wheels that have the most influence in forcing the leading flanges up to the outside of a curve.

# How Railways Affected Life in Britain

Railways had a great effect on life in Britain. The Industrial Revolution increased the demand for the movement both of raw materials and manufactured goods to markets at home and abroad. Roads were unsuitable and canals expensive as they lacked competition.

Towns had developed due to industry, and because their inhabitants were unable to collect firewood from trees or grow their own food, fuel and food had to be brought to them; the railway was ideal for this. In pre-railway years, much of London's food originated from a belt of market gardens where the inner suburbs now stand. Fresh meat was scarce and expensive, while milk was often tubercular, coming from cows kept actually in the city.

Railways tended to demarcate towns, with industry on one side of the line and residential areas and shops on the other, or a line might divide high-class from lower-class dwellings.

Although railways gave farmers a wider market, they had disadvantages: a line through property may have left some fields too small to be economic; a railway reduced accessibility from one side to another despite the provision of level crossings or cattle creeps; and a railway's earthworks could affect drainage.

Railways allowed heavy building materials to be transported easily and cheaply, so many a middle-class home of the Victorian period was of red brick, faced with freestone, roofed with slate and crowned by ridge tiles, all probably transported by rail.

Transport had hitherto been by a coach or wagon worked by two men, or, if a barge, by a family. On the other hand, a railway needed an army of men: station staff, train staff, permanent way staff and factory staff.

Opening railways affected the employment of many people. It caused the cessation of most horse coach services, leaving drivers, guards, ostlers, farriers, saddlers, feed merchants and innkeepers either jobless or with less trade. Likewise, the canals were far less busy. On the other hand, the railways created employment, first through their construction and then in running them, and often these were jobs which demanded more education than those they displaced.

A railway offered a more dependable form of transport when time was of the essence because, in the case of ships, some vessels only linked one port with another annually, and then it was vital not to miss the boat. Canals could be unreliable in times of ice or drought.

Railways encouraged far more people to hold shares as they could easily be purchased by small investors, especially since shares in a new railway were not generally 'paid up' but bought by a deposit, generally of about 10 per cent, the rest promised when later 'calls' were made as the building of the line progressed. This caused companies trouble, as some investors speculated and purchased shares, hoping to sell them at a profit before calls were made. If calls could not be met, the shares were forfeited.

Railways were also the first large joint-stock companies, with the capital consisting largely of small holdings of shares owned by the general public, for, until 1825, joint-stock companies had been illegal under the Bubble Act of 1720, which was passed to prevent a repetition of the South Sea Bubble.

Until the coming of railways, most people had no holidays as we think of them today, only the occasional saint's day or fair day. The majority of workers never travelled beyond the borders of their own parish. As industrial towns grew, so too did the need to escape from them for a holiday – first by the middle class and then the working class. Railways met this growing need. In 1835, a single ticket for travelling from London to Brighton by coach cost £1 1s 0d inside or 12s outside, the journey taking six hours. In 1844, the rail fare was 14s 6d first class, 9s 6d second and 4s 2d third class, the journey taking two and a half hours. In 1846, one Brighton excursion consisted of forty-four coaches drawn by four locomotives and carried 4,000 passengers.

A day by the sea was a Victorian worker's dream of heaven. To discourage trippers, some select watering places, such as Sidmouth, decreed that their stations should be some distance from the sea.

One of the first railway excursions was on 5 July 1841. Organised by Thomas Cook, it carried around a thousand temperance supporters from Leicester to Loughborough. The fare for 11 miles return, including sandwiches, tea, dancing and games, was one shilling. In 1850, return day trips from London to Brighton, Dover, Hastings, or Margate cost 3s 6d. A great catalyst for rail travel was the Great Exhibition held in Hyde Park in 1851. There were 19,000 exhibits in the Crystal Palace, which was twice the width and four times the length of St Paul's Cathedral. It attracted visitors from all over the country; in fact, numbers attending equalled a third of the population of England and Wales. Without railways, it would have been impossible to bring together the exhibits or carry such numbers of visitors. By 1851, almost every important town in England had a rail link to the capital. Special excursion fares to visit the exhibition were within the pocket of all but the poorest, and some businesses offered employees and their families free trips.

Subscription clubs were established to enable the working class to pay fares by instalments, and the normal single third-class fare of 15s from Manchester and Leeds to London was lowered to the excursion rate of 5s return; that is, a day's wages for a craftsman, two days' wages for an urban labourer and at a price within reach of all but the very poor. All this contrasted with the state of affairs two decades earlier, when travel on the outside of a stagecoach would have cost £1 15s 0d single, with no possibility of a day return as the journey just one way took at least nineteen hours.

Some of the excursion trains were of immense length. In 1852, the West Cornwall Railway ran a teetotallers' trip from Redruth and Camborne to Hayle consisting of three locomotives and seventy-five broad gauge coaches. A song was written for the occasion, with the rousing chorus:

> Happy Camborne, happy Camborne,
> Where the railway is so near,
> And the engine shows how water
> Can accomplish more than beer.

A paper reported that, on the return journey, the locomotives ran out of steam and stopped beside an orchard: 'It may have been their extreme anxiety to take measures against such an intoxicating beverage as cider, but at all events that army of teetotallers swarmed down from the trucks and up the apple trees until the orchard resembled the famous cupboard of Mother Hubbard.'

The coming of railways saved both time and money. In 1841, Cecil Torr's father travelled from London to Exeter by coach in twenty-one hours. In October 1842, he travelled as far as Taunton by train and arrived at Exeter in only twelve and a quarter hours. In March 1845, he took ten and a quarter hours going the whole way by train, while in 1846 the express took only six and a half hours. The horse-drawn coach fare for London to Exeter varied between £3 and £3 10s, to which about a quarter had to be added in tips, but the railway fare was only £2 4s 6d first class or £2 10s od express, and no tips were required.

Before the general use of the telegraph, the railway was responsible for bringing the very latest Continental news. *The Times* and *The Herald* each paid £10 every twenty-four hours to maintain an engine in steam at Dover, ready to rush the latest news to London.

Queen Victoria was initially reluctant to use the railway, even though Prince Albert and Dowager Queen Adelaide had done so several times. Eventually Albert persuaded her to give it a try, and at noon on 13 June 1842 the queen, Prince Albert and their suite left Slough for Paddington, the chief locomotive engineer, Daniel Gooch, driving the engine *Phlegethon*. She told her uncle Leopold, King of the Belgians, that the journey was free from dust, crowd and heat and that she was quite charmed with it.

Not everyone was happy with the queen using this form of transport, and Colonel Sibthorp, MP for Lincoln, asked a question in the Commons about the royal person being exposed to such peril. Her majesty had faith in the railway, and ten days later she returned by train to Slough, taking with her the infant Prince of Wales, later to be King Edward VII. She enjoyed fifty-nine years of railway travel and it enabled her to travel to other residences which she purchased at Balmoral, Osborne and Sandringham. She insisted on the speed being restricted to 40 mph, and it was ironic that her funeral train from Gosport to Victoria station, leaving late, was ordered by King Edward VII to try and regain time. It raced through Chichester at 80 mph – twice the speed at which she travelled during her lifetime.

Along with the six-wheeler on the South Eastern, Queen Victoria's eight-wheeled carriage on the Great Western was the first in Britain to have a toilet – most necessary when her journeys began and ended with ceremony and offered no opportunity for discreet withdrawal. In 1869, the London & North Western built her a pair of carriages for day and night travel respectively and these were the very first British coaches to be linked by a closed, flexible gangway.

By 1851, for the first time in *any* country, more people in England lived in towns than in the country. In 1801, there were only fifteen towns with a population of over 20,000; by 1851, there were sixty-three. Between 1851 and 1891 the urban population grew from 50 to 72 per cent of the total, and in 1891 some 185 towns had a population of over 20,000. Some railways set up new towns themselves for their works – Crewe, Swindon and Wolverton, for example – and developed resorts such as Blackpool, Bournemouth and Eastbourne. Trains could carry as many passengers in a week as the stagecoaches carried in a year. Railways bringing cheap coal enabled water mills to change from their unreliable source of power to dependable steam. They also brought great benefit to the working class, who could now travel to new jobs while still visiting the family at their birth place.

Railway companies looked after their employees. For example, the London & North Western Railway at Crewe built houses with a rental of 2*s* to 4*s* 3*d* a week according to size. It provided a church and school, paying the curate and schoolmaster; it paid for two policemen to keep order in the town; a medical doctor was available on insurance at the cost of 1*d* week for a single man and 2*d* a week for a family. The company supplied water, emptied cesspits, collected rubbish and provided allotments and a savings bank. Crewe had a population of 203 before the coming of the railway; it then grew to 4,571 in 1851, and 42,074 in 1901.

In 1871, Sir John Lubbock's Act made Boxing Day, Easter and Whit Monday and the first Monday in August statutory bank holidays, and railways offered excursions on these days. Paid holidays for manual workers were rare before 1880 and were not the norm until after the Second World War. In the last quarter of the nineteenth century, the better-paid working class had more money to spend on such luxuries as day trips and holidays; some were very adventurous. In 1900, Messrs Lever Brothers took 1,600 employees and families on a two-day excursion to the Paris Exhibition; this required four trains. On 22 July 1900, 22,500 in one day enjoyed the Great Western Railway 'Trip' given to the GWR's Swindon employees.

Prior to the building of its suburban railways, London only stretched about 4 miles in radius from Charing Cross, yet by 1901 the development of railways had formed Greater London, which spread over an area ten times as large, while some season ticket holders travelled from as far afield as Brighton and Southend.

Commuting also took place in the provinces: Birmingham factory owners lived and enjoyed fresh air in Solihull, or Stratford-upon-Avon; those from Bristol resided at Bath, Clevedon or

Weston-super-Mare; Liverpool merchants lived at New Brighton, Southport or West Kirby and Manchester traders at Alderley Edge, Altrincham or Wilmslow, while those at Newcastle had homes at Hexham or Tynemouth. Poorer workers could not afford money for fares and so lived within walking distance of work.

Some suburbs were strung along railway lines – Metroland being a fine example. To aid such development, railways offered season tickets to white-collar workers and workmen's cheap returns to those of a lower class. Glasgow provided the reverse of the normal pattern: industry developed on the outskirts of the city, the city itself being a dormitory, with trains carrying passengers out in the morning and inwards in the evening. Birmingham also had trains running outwards to Cadbury's at Bournville.

London's main stations, particularly on the north side where property was more expensive, were placed on the edge of the built-up area: Euston (1837), Paddington (1838) and King's Cross (1852). To increase the number of passengers using Euston, the London & North Western offered an eleven-year free pass for anyone taking a house with an annual rental minimum of £50 and a twenty-one year lease at Tring and Leighton, but few accepted this offer. The problem was that the streets between Euston and the City were too crowded and it took a long time to travel from the railway terminus to the City.

The Great Western and the Great Northern provided the solution by setting up the Metropolitan Railway – the world's first underground line. Opened from Paddington and King's Cross to Farringdon Street in the City in 1863, it was extended to Moorgate in 1865.

It was built just below street level by the expedient of making a street into a huge trench, covering it with a brick arch and then relaying the road on top. As steam engines were used, provision was made for ventilation. Exhaust from the engines was condensed. Flaps worked by rods from the footplate sent exhaust steam up the chimney when working in the open, or directed it into the tanks when in a tunnel. The water in the tanks became overheated, and very often it was necessary to exhaust steam into air in the tunnel.

This happened all too frequently, and on 7 October 1884 *The Times*, reporting a journey from King's Cross to Baker Street, likened it to 'a mild form of torture which no sane person would undergo if he could help it'. Although the purity of the air in tunnels and stations left something to be desired, the underground railway proved popular and certainly speeded passengers from A to B. Despite all these fumes issuing from its locomotives, curiously, the Metropolitan banned smoking in its coaches, though this ruling was overturned in 1874 as a belated result of an amendment to the Railway Regulation Act of 1868, which required all railways to provide a smoking carriage on every train.

In 1863, the Select Committee of the House of Lords recommended linking all London main-line termini by underground to form a circle line. This was not completed by the District Railway until 1884. The Metropolitan and the District railways proved rivals, and in 1884 the latter chained a train to a disputed siding and the Metropolitan sent three locomotives to try and remove it. They were unsuccessful.

To the north-east of London, the Great Eastern Railway pursued an active policy of developing suburban lines serving Liverpool Street and won more commuters than any other railway. To achieve parliamentary assent to its 1861 Act to create its Liverpool Street terminus, it was forced to provide workmen's trains at 2*d* return for journeys up to 10 miles. This was a contrast to the Great Western and London & North Western, which actively discouraged lower-class commuters by offering no, or only a few, cheap trains at an early hour.

Most of the British trunk lines were built in the first half of the nineteenth century, and the second half saw the arrival of a plethora of small local companies, very often proving unprofitable and eventually being purchased by larger companies at less-than-cost price. The second half of the century also saw engineering marvels such as the Midland's Settle & Carlisle, built by 6,000 navvies across the Pennines and opened in 1876; the Severn Tunnel opened in 1887, and the Forth Bridge in 1890.

**WIRRAL RAILWAY.**

This Ticket is issued subject to the conditions stated on the Co's Time Bills.

**THIRD CLASS**

WEST KIRBY To

# MORETON

6619

Fare 4d.     MORETON

Ulverston                    FURNESS RY

**BOWNESS** To

# ULVERSTON

By STEAMER & RAIL

Available on day of issue only

**THIRD CLASS**

FARE 1/9½

9543

This Ticket is issued subject to the Company's Bye-Laws, Regulations, and to the Conditions in the Time Tables, Books, Bills, and Notices, it is available only to and from the stations named thereon, and its transfer is an indictable fraud.

Bowness          **FURNESS RLY**

**THIRD CLASS**

ULVERSTON

TO

# BOWNESS

BY RAIL & STEAMER

Available on day of issue only.

OVER                FARE 1/9½

4327

# 6

# Signalling

The earliest form of signalling was given by policemen, who showed 'All Right' by holding the left arm horizontally towards the road indicated, 'Caution' by lifting it above the head and 'Stop' by raising both hands. In the later 1830s, pivoted boards appeared. Many companies used disc-and-crossbar signals – a disc indicating 'Clear', and a crossbar 'Stop'. The Croydon Railway used the semaphore type of signal derived from naval and military use and the South Eastern and the London & Brighton also adopted this pattern in 1842. An arm at right angles to the post indicated 'Stop', lowered 45 degrees meant 'Proceed with Caution' and when it fell within a slot in the post this meant 'All Clear'. The equivalent lights at night were red, green and white. Signals were placed at 'Clear' five minutes after a train had passed, the time being measured by a sandglass.

The system was hazardous, as a train could well have broken down round a curve just out of sight of the policeman. In the event of a train stalling within a section, its guard was required to go back and lay detonators on the rail and exhibit a red flag or lamp. Trains in those early days did not carry headlamps, as *The Railway Companion* published in 1833 explained that 'the fire of the engine is sufficient to give warning to the policeman or to any object upon the road of the approach of a train'. The same book described a revolving rear lamp, red on one side and blue on the other, which presented a red light while the train was in motion and a blue one on coming to a stand, but unfortunately does not reveal how this was achieved.

In 1856, John Saxby took out a patent for a mechanism whereby signals and points were operated by one lever, thus ensuring that signals and points could not indicate a conflicting movement.

The electric telegraph, invented by Cooke & Wheatstone in 1837, made it possible to inform when a train had left a station. This enabled the time interval method to be replaced by the block system, whereby a train was not allowed to enter a length of line until the previous train had vacated it. The first railway to be worked completely on the block system in conjunction with the telegraph was the Yarmouth & Norwich in 1844. Its use gradually spread to other railways, though some were reluctant to spend money on wiring every signal box.

The London, Brighton & South Coast had a mixture of time interval on open parts of the line and the block system in tunnels. This mixture was the main cause of the Clayton Tunnel disaster of 25 August 1861 when twenty-three people were killed. When the Board of Trade inspecting officer criticised the company for failing to adopt block working throughout, the directors replied that 'they still fear that the telegraphic system of working recommended by the Board of Trade will, by transferring much responsibility from the engine drivers, augment rather than diminish the risk of accident'.

The London, Chatham & Dover Railway was the first company to install the Sykes system of electric block signalling. The signal at A box was locked at danger until the signalman at the next box, B, operated an electric current to release the lock. To prevent any mistake, a treadle was inserted in the line between B and C, and once B had accepted a train from A, he could not release the lock until the train had passed B's box, and worked the treadle on its way to C.

Railways in Britain were initially run by independent companies, having little contact with others. Then, as the network developed, the need developed for some sort of over-arching group to make provision for through booking over the lines of several companies and for the transit of 'foreign' wagons over lines, and then, with running over other companies' lines, it was necessary that buffers, couplings and brakes should be standardised.

The result was that representatives of nine companies met on 2 January 1842 to form the Railway Clearing House (RCH). Membership was voluntary, and some principal railways, such as the Great Western, stayed aloof until the early 1860s, but most joined by 1870. The RCH had as principal objectives:

a) To organise the through booking of passengers.
b) To organise the through booking of personally owned horses and carriages.
c) To divide passenger receipts on a mileage basis.
d) To encourage through transport of goods on a mileage basis.
e) To provide that all debts between companies be settled at the RCH.

The RCH set up a debtor and creditor account with all the railways and the balance due to each paid at the end of every month. Freight charges could be quite complex. First came the terminal charges, credited equally to the terminus of collection or reception and the terminus of delivery, the rest of the sum divided between the companies according to mileage. The company in ownership of the wagon, which may or may not have been the originating company, was also entitled to a share. If a consignment or wagon became damaged, then costs needed to be apportioned.

From 1847, the RCH employed number takers to check the numbers and contents of wagons travelling on 'foreign' lines. In September 1847, the RCH recommended that member companies adopt Greenwich time rather than local time. This was essential due to the speed of rail travel. Hitherto, the longest land journey in England was London to Plymouth in twenty-two hours by stagecoach, and the fact that local time was twenty minutes later than London was of no consequence. In 1841, the Leeds to Rugby Railway used Greenwich time but the London & Birmingham adopted local time, hence confusion when transferring from one system to another at Rugby. With the introduction of the electric telegraph, enabling time signals to be sent, by 1852 Greenwich time was adopted by all railways.

In 1914 the RCH employed a staff of over 3,000, but the simplification caused by the 1923 Grouping caused employment to fall to 1,800 by September 1939. Nationalisation in 1948 simplified matters even more, and the RCH was eventually disbanded on 31 March 1963.

Thomas Edmondson invented the standard railway ticket, which remained in general use until February 1990. He prepared serially numbered tickets ready for sale. Trained as a cabinetmaker before being appointed stationmaster on the Newcastle & Carlisle, he designed a wooden press for dating the tickets through an inked ribbon. In association with John Blaylock, a Carlisle clockmaker and iron founder, he devised an iron date press and a ticket-printing machine – early tickets had been written by hand. From the 1840s most railways adopted his system, paying him an annual royalty of 10s a mile.

35. Royal Scot class 4-6-0 No. 6144 *Ostrich*, named after a locomotive of 1842 designed by John Dewrance. (Author's collection)

36. There's no danger of ex-Great Eastern Railway 0-4-0ST LNER No. 8081 running short of coal! (Author's collection)

37. Ex-North Eastern Railway LNER 0-4-0T No. 986 is designed for shunting sidings where curves are sharp. It resembles a child's clockwork toy. (Author's collection)

38. Ex-Great Central Railway 4-4-0 as LNER No. 5104 *Queen Alexandra* at Brunswick, Cheshire Lines committee shed, July 1937. (W. Potter)

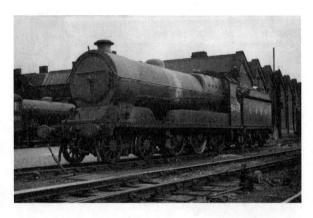

39. Ex-Great Central Railway 4-6-0 No 5442 at Annesley shed, July 1937. (W. Potter)

40. Ex-Great Central Railway 0-6-2T as BR No 69311. Notice the unusually long side tanks with a gap for access to oil the inside motion. (Author's collection)

41. SR 0-4-4T No. W18 *Wingwood* stands over an inspection pit at Ryde shed on the Isle of Wight. The Westinghouse brake pump can be seen beside the smoke box and the air tank is above the side tank. Part of a water crane is on the far left. The notice attached to it reads, 'No shunting or shunt movements to be made beyond this point.' (Author's collection)

42. The streamlined LMS 4-6-2 No. 6220 *Coronation*. (Author's collection)

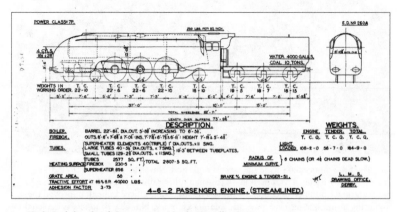

43. Technical details of *Coronation*. (Author's collection)

44. The semi-streamlined GWR 4-6-0 No. 6014 *King Henry VII* climbs through Ashley Hill with the Up Bristolian, 15 June 1936. (Author's collection)

45. The un-streamlined No. 6000 *King George V.* (Author's collection)

46. The SR Schools class were the newest and most powerful 4-4-0s in Britain, introduced by Richard Maunsell in 1930 when other railways had changed to designs with a greater number of coupled wheels. His successor, Oliver Bulleid, improved them by fitting a multiple-jet blast pipe and a larger chimney. No. 923 *Bradfield* is depicted here. (W. Potter)

47. Terrier 0-6-0T No. 32661 leaves Havant for Hayling Island around 1960. The engine is dwarfed by its coaches. It is slung so low that half the buffers are above the buffer beam. This class was needed as a bridge on the branch had a severe weight restriction. (Revd Alan Newman)

48. Although it has the appearance of a diesel engine, No. 47191 is actually a steamer. The vertical boiler is placed in the cab and gearing is below the bonnet. The coal hopper can be seen above the number 47191. Having a short wheelbase and low height, it was very useful in certain circumstances. Seen here at Derby on 29 April 1952 after overhaul, it was normally seen at Radstock. (R. J. Buckley)

49. GWR 0-6-0ST No. 2007 at Worcester shed, 8 October 1949; it was withdrawn two months later. When going backwards, a storm sheet between cab and bunker offered a certain amount of protection. It was one of the few GWR saddle tanks never converted to a pannier tank. (W. Potter)

50. An SR firefighting 0-4-2T fitted with a water pump. (Author's collection)

51. Some LMS Class 8F 2-8-0s were built for the War Department. Here No. 41.181 of the Iranian State Railway is waiting to leave Arak with a Down train of empties. (E. J. M. Hayward)

52. Other 2-8-0s were supplied by the American Locomotive Company. Here S160 class No. 1604 stands outside 'A' shop at Swindon, having been modified by the GWR, to which it was loaned from January 1943 to September 1944. (Author's collection)

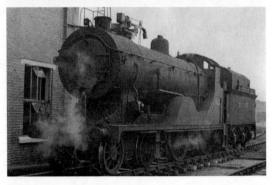

53. SR 4-4-0 No. 463, fitted for oil burning, the tender holding an oil tank in addition to the usual water supply. It is fitted with electric lighting. (Author's collection)

54 (*bottom*). Ex-LMS 4-4-0 No. 666, seen here in early BR days with the temporary 'British Railways' on its tender and 'M' (for London Midland Region) prefix to its LMS number. (Author's collection)

55. In due course prefixes were abolished and all engines, except those of the GWR, were renumbered. Here, ex-LMS rebuilt Royal Scot class 4-6-0 No. 6124 *London Scottish* receives a new cast plate with an additional '4'. 8A is the shed code for Edge Hill, Liverpool. (Author's collection)

56. Ex-GWR outside-cylinder 0-6-0PT No. 1368 (82F, Weymouth shed) at Custom House Quay on the Weymouth Tramway in June 1955, with a van train of Channel Islands produce. (Author's collection)

57. Bulleid's air-smoothed Pacific No. 35021 *New Zealand Line*, seen here at Weymouth on 30 August 1953. The thermic siphons, Boxpok wheels and chain-driven valve gear were some of its unusual features; the raised coaling stage can be seen beyond. (Revd Alan Newman)

58. To obviate the problems of the Merchant Navy class, the engines were rebuilt. No. 35016 *Elders Fyffes* is shown here at Eastleigh on 5 October 1962. A Schools class 4-4-0 stands behind. (Revd Alan Newman)

59. A lighter version, the West Country/Battle of Britain class, appeared, No. 34106 *Lydford* being an example and seen here at Salisbury, 18 October 1962. (Revd Alan Newman)

60. Most of the West Country/ Battle of Britain class were similarly rebuilt, such as No. 34100 *Appledore*, seen here at Brighton, 12 August 1962. (Revd Alan Newman)

61. Ex-Somerset & Dorset Railway 2-8-0 No. 53804 (82F, Bath, Green Park) near its home shed. Although designed for heavy freight work by Sir Henry Fowler of the Midland, the MR never built any for its own use, preferring to use relatively small 0-6-0s. (Revd Alan Newman)

62. Ex-LNWR 0-8-0 No. 48930 (21B Bescot) at its home shed on 6 June 1962. These were very useful heavy-freight locomotives. No. 48930, unlike most of its sisters, has a tender cab. (Revd Alan Newman)

63. Ex-GWR 2-8-0 No. 4705 on 26 September 1961 at Bristol Temple Meads, waiting to move a Down freight. These large-boilered, mixed-traffic locomotives were chiefly used on fast night-freight workings and were only occasionally seen in daylight. (Revd Alan Newman)

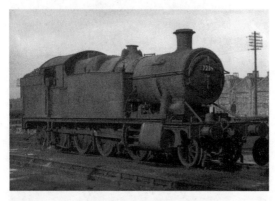

64. Ex-GWR 2-8-2T No. 7239 at Oxford on 4 September 1962. These heavy freight engines, with a capacity of 6 tons of coal and 2,500 gallons of water, were not far short of a tender engine's 7 tons and 3,500 gallons. (Revd Alan Newman)

65. Ex-LMS Class 8F 2-8-0 No. 48602 (21B Bescot) at its home shed on 26 April 1962. Unusually, it has a Fowler tender rather than a high-sided Stanier one. It was built by the SR at Eastleigh in 1943. (Revd Alan Newman)

66. Ex-GWR 4-4-0 No. 9017 stored at Aberystwyth on 25 May 1959. Relatively light, it was built in 1938 using Bulldog class frames and a Duke class boiler. (Revd Alan Newman)

67. BR Standard Class 4 2-6-0 No. 76060. 'SC' on the smoke box door indicates that it has a self-cleaning smoke box and ashes do not need to be shovelled out. The locomotive is designed for easy maintenance and the motion accessible for oiling. The track is electrified. (Author's collection)

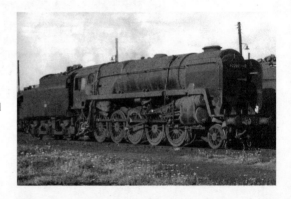

68. The BR Standard Class 9 2-10-0s proved magnificent machines; although intended for freight, they could speed a passenger train up to 90 mph. This example, No. 92207, is seen at Oxford on 4 September 1962. (Author's collection)

**FURNESS RLY**
PRIVILEGE RETURN
Available for one journey
only within One Month
of issue.
Not Transferable
THIRD CLASS
Ambleside
TO
BOWNESS
88
Turnover    Ambles

824

Cheshire Lines Co
Return on day of issue
or following day
WEST DERBY to
**LIVERPOOL Centl**
FIRST CLASS
Fare 1s

26 FE 93    CHESHIRE LINES COMMITTEE
Issued subject to the Regulations & Condi-
tions stated in the Co's Time Tables & Bills.
AVAILABLE ON DAY OF ISSUE ONLY
Liverpool Central to (V)
**ST. MICHAEL'S**
7722
Third Class    St. Mich.    Fare 2½d

# 7

# Railways in Late Victorian Times

As Scotland has a much-indented coastline, it was necessary for some of its railways either to build major bridges or to have ferries, with the time-wasting and bother of unloading goods and passengers and transferring from rail to steamer or vice versa.

Dundee could be reached from Edinburgh by rail via Perth, but the direct route required a ferry or bridge across the Firth of Forth and the River Tay. The economic success of the Edinburgh, Perth & Dundee Railway as a viable through route depended entirely on the efficient operation of the two ferries, and violent storms in those estuaries were not unknown. In due course, these ferries were purchased by the railway company. They proved particularly unsatisfactory for goods cartage, as traffic needed to be manhandled on or off the boats four times on the 50 miles between Edinburgh and Dundee. These boats were often out of commission for long periods as their crew lacked the expertise to maintain and repair them. The Edinburgh, Perth & Dundee just could not compete with the all-land line in the through carriage of heavy loads such as minerals and timber. Then, in 1849, Thomas Bouch was appointed engineer and manager of the company.

He corrected the ferries' minor faults and then made a brilliant suggestion – a train ferry to carry wagons across the Forth. A hinged section of track would link the land part of the line to the track on the ferry, thus allowing for the tidal range of approximately 20 feet.

Although the world's first train ferry, the *Leviathan,* was built and ready by September 1849, Bouch was slow at finishing his onshore rail installation, so she was unable to enter service until 1 March 1850. She was able to carry thirty-four wagons, which hitherto had travelled by the rival route. Bouch's idea increased the company's dividends and won him an associateship of the Institute of Civil Engineers. He resigned from the railway and set up business as a consulting engineer.

Although the train ferry was successful, it was felt that a bridge across the Forth would be even better. The problem was that wide mudflats and a mud-filled ancient channel beneath the riverbed made tunnelling or creating the foundations for a pier difficult. Bouch proposed two high-level suspension bridges with a pier on the islet of Inchgarvie, but work on the Tay Bridge had priority.

The North British Railway, which had absorbed the Edinburgh, Perth & Dundee in 1862, could only reach Dundee by ferry from Tayport, this taking a minimum of three hours and twenty minutes for a journey of 46 six miles when the weather was favourable.

Bouch proposed a bridge across the Tay, and the shareholders were excited that Scotland would possess the longest bridge in the world. Unfortunately, they did not realise that Bouch was really a very inefficient engineer. He had been appointed consulting engineer to many small railway companies, but had overlooked many deficiencies: one had timber bridges of inadequate dimensions made with untreated wood, the rails on the line had been insecurely fixed and the sleepers laid at 4-foot instead of 3-foot intervals. Another railway engineered by Bouch found its track was substandard; level crossing gates failed to close properly and an engine pit lacked drainage and was too small for a man to enter.

The Act for the Tay Bridge was passed in 1870. The contract having been placed in 1871 and the first train crossing on 26 September 1877, Bouch received a knighthood for his work. Even with the ferry crossing across the Forth, the journey time from Aberdeen to Edinburgh was reduced from seven hours and thirty-five minutes to four hours fifty-five minutes, meaning that, for the first time ever, a return trip could be made in a day. To provide recompense for the cost of the bridge, the North British was allowed to reckon its length for charging purposes as 6 miles, this figure later being changed to 10 miles.

Then, on 28 December 1879, tragedy struck – the bridge collapsed under the last train of the day. All seventy-five passengers and train crew on board died, making this the only British railway accident where no passenger survived.

Subsequent investigation showed that imperfect castings for the bridge had been delivered, with holes and cracks filled with Beaumont egg, a concoction of carbon and wax; that nobody knew that concrete had burst the iron columns it filled; that trains had crossed the bridge at speeds over 40 mph when the restriction was 25 mph; that maintenance was in the charge of a man whose experience was in bricklaying; and that Bouch had made no allowance for wind speed, which at times reached 90 mph. Sir Thomas Bouch died ten months after the collapse of his bridge.

4-4-0 No. 224 lay on the bottom of the river for three months. Only slightly damaged, it was put on the rails at Tayport and travelled on its own wheels to Cowlairs, where it was repaired and set to work again.

One would have thought that No. 224 had gone through enough adventures to be allowed to end its days in peace, but in the compounding epidemic of the 1880s No. 224 was rebuilt as a four-cylinder compound. The extra cost of upkeep and repairs proved greater than the cost of the fuel saved, so it reverted to its previous 'simple' condition.

A new Tay Bridge was approved in 1881 with a formation 60 yards west of the old structure and some of the old girders recycled, though the new bridge had double track rather than single. Opened on 11 July 1887, it is over 2 miles in length and consists of eighty-five spans, the widest with a span of 245 feet.

Work on the Forth Bridge did not start until 1878, but then, following the Tay Bridge disaster, work ceased. Bouch's plans being completely out of fashion, the idea of having suspension bridges was dropped in favour of Benjamin Baker's cantilever design, which incorporated girders from the old design into the new structure as outside girders in the approach spans. The bridge is 1½ miles long, while the two main spans each measure 1,710 feet, making them the longest in the world at the time of their erection. It was the first major British bridge to be built of steel, as opposed to wrought iron, thus allowing a much greater span.

The Forth Bridge Railway Committee was set up and the bridge paid for by a consortium of several companies: the North British contributed 35 per cent, the Midland 30 per cent and the remaining 35 per cent was shared equally by the Great Northern and North Eastern.

The contractor, William Arrol, devised a new method of constructing the main girders. Instead of them being built on shore and floated on barges to be raised into position, they were built out from the ends of the cantilever arms to meet midway.

Some 4,600 workers were employed at peak time, and sixty-three men lost their lives during its construction. It opened on 4 March 1890, and, for charging purposes, the bridge was reckoned as 10 miles.

With the opening of the Forth Bridge traffic through Edinburgh, Waverley station grew enormously and proved too inadequate to cope; its main platform was approached by only double track and the platform was just 4 feet wide. Sometimes, through traffic could take an hour to cover 6 miles. *The Times* commented that trains were late into Plymouth due to delays at Edinburgh the previous day! E. Foxwell and T. C. Farrer, in *Express Trains: English and Foreign*, published in 1888, give a description of the turbulence:

On the platforms of the Waverley station at Edinburgh may be witnessed every evening in summer a scene of confusion so chaotic that a sober description of it is incredible to those who have not themselves survived it. Trains of caravan length come in portentously late from Perth, so that each is mistaken for its successor; these have to be broken up and remade on insufficient sidings, while the bewildered crowds of tourists sway up and down amongst equally bewildered porters on the narrow village platform reserved for these most important expresses; the higher officials stand lost in subtle thought, returning now and then to repeated enquiries some masterpiece of reply couched in the cautious conditional, while the hands of the clock with a humorous air survey the abandoned sight, till at length without any obvious reason and with sudden stealth, the shame-stricken driver hurries his passengers off into the dark. Once off, the driver and the engine do much to make us forget the disgraceful rout from which we have just emerged, for the North British engines, especially those which work the Midland trains to and from Carlisle, achieve some of the very best express running in the world – over such hills.

Waverley was rebuilt and 6 miles of approach track quadrupled between 1892 and 1900. One driver was on duty seventeen hours a day for a whole month solely due to goods trains being delayed waiting for a path through Waverley.

Another cantilever bridge in Scotland spans Loch Etive at Connel Ferry. Strong tidal currents prevented the building of a central pier, so a cantilever design with a span of 500 feet was adopted and became the Forth Bridge's biggest British rival. The entire length of the bridge and its approaches is 1,044 ft. Construction started in 1898 and was completed in 1903. During working hours, a rowing boat was in constant attendance to rescue anyone who fell. It was used on at least one occasion when it rescued a rivet lad who fell 50 feet.

Connell Ferry Bridge was unusual due to the fact that it was designed for use also by road traffic. Due to contention with the local authority over tolls, for the first few years of existence road vehicles were carried on a flat truck which was drawn over the bridge by a tractor adapted for rail use. Eventually a road was laid close to the railway, and, when no train was signalled, vehicles crossed under their own power. Gates were provided at each end, interlocked with signals like a level crossing. As the bridge saved a 35-mile detour, the toll was relatively high. When the branch closed in 1966, it became a single-lane bridge.

The longest English railway bridge, and third in the whole British Isles behind those spanning the Tay and the Forth, was the Severn Bridge. The first stone of the 4,162-foot-long bridge was laid on 3 June 1875 and it opened to traffic on 17 October 1879, curiously enough exactly a century after the first iron bridge in the world was constructed, which was also built across the Severn.

The Severn Bridge consisted of a series of iron bow-string girders resting on cast-iron piers filled with concrete and rock. It was jointly owned by the Midland and Great Western railways, giving the former company valuable access to coal in the Forest of Dean.

An interesting feature of the bridge was that it had a swing span over the Gloucester & Berkeley Canal. An engine driver was required to be on duty on one of the day shifts in order to maintain the engine and machinery operating the span in good order, the signalman on the other shift assisting in cleaning and coaling. As the swing span was left open at night, the man on early turn was required to have the engine in steam ready for swinging the span at least twenty minutes before the first train was due. The man on late turn was responsible for banking the fire after the last train of the day had passed and the swing span opened. The two boilers were used alternately for a fortnight, one being in use while the other was washed out.

The opening of the Severn Tunnel in 1886 somewhat eclipsed the bridge, but on winter Sundays, when the civil engineer had complete possession of the tunnel, trains were diverted across the bridge. The largest engines permitted to cross it were Dean Goods 0-6-0s, and as a result this class was not scrapped as quickly as it might have been.

During the Second World War, it was not unknown for pilots on training flights to dive planes between the bridge deck and the water. An onlooker admired them until he saw men painting the bridge, hanging in their cradle while an aircraft flew within a few feet of them!

The end of the bridge came on 25 October 1960, when it was

struck by an oil tanker which destroyed two spans. Unfortunately for British Railways, under the Merchant Shipping Act, the limited liability for damage through collision did not exceed the sum equal to about twenty-four times the net registered tonnage of the vessel, so BR only received £5,000, a quite inadequate sum to repair the damage. In 1967, the bridge was dismantled.

Another great British bridge was the Britannia Bridge, built to carry the Holyhead line across the Menai Strait. As there was only one suitable rock for intermediate support, Robert Stephenson had to provide spans in excess of 450 feet. Cast-iron arches were ruled out as causing an obstruction to sailing ships, while a normal suspension bridge was too flexible for a railway.

He solved the problem by using two stiff wrought-iron tubes, the tubes being rectangular with cellular tops and bottoms for greater strength. The single-span Conway Bridge used this design and opened in 1848, followed by the Britannia Bridge in 1850. Unfortunately, in 1970 the cover of the Britannia Bridge caught fire and the heat caused the bridge to sag. It was replaced by a combined road and rail bridge, and arches could then be used due to there being almost no tall sailing vessels.

Another important bridge was the Royal Albert Bridge at Saltash, carrying the railway across the Tamar from Devon into Cornwall. Here the river was 1,100 feet wide and 70 feet deep in the centre at high water and the Admiralty demanded clearance for sailing vessels. Brunel opted for one pier and two spans of 455 feet. He believed that a short single section of railway would not seriously delay traffic and that building the bridge for single track, rather than double, would save a minimum of £100,000.

Work started by sinking a cylinder to obtain a foundation for the central pier, the men inside having to work in a pressure of

*Above right:*
69. Road and
rail transport at
Rainhill, 1831. (T.
T. Bury)

*Right:* 70. Euston
station, 1837. Most
of the coaches
on the far left are
open. The closed
coach has a luggage
rack on its roof. (T.
T. Bury)

*Below:* 71. Water
and rail traffic
at Canal Bridge,
King's Langley,
1837. (T. T. Bury)

72. The first-class coach *Experience* of the Liverpool & Manchester Railway owes much to stagecoach design. The image is one of many produced by the London & North Western Railway. (Author's collection)

73. The GWR 4-2-2 *Lord of the Isles*, built in 1851. The leading and trailing wheels are fixed to the frame. The tender carries a seat for the travelling porter who ensured that all was well with the train. (Author's collection)

74. Gooch's broad gauge 2-4-0T at Praed Street on the Metropolitan Railway. It was the first British locomotive to be fitted with condensing apparatus and had outside cylinders. Notice the mixed gauge tracks. (Author's collection)

*Above right:* 75. The last Down broad gauge Flying Dutchman, 20 May 1892. (Author's collection)

*Below right:* 76. This oil-fired Great Eastern Railway royal engine 2-4-0 has No. 751 on the cabside plate, though the colour artist has painted the wrong number on its buffer beam. It was built in 1886 and this picture was made before 1908, when it was rebuilt as a 4-4-0. (Author's collection)

77. A GWR London to Birmingham express hauled by a Duke class 4-4-0. (Author's collection)

78. South Eastern & Chatham Railway 4-4-0 No. 482. (Author's collection)

79. Cambrian Railways 4-4-0 No. 81. (Author's collection)

80. Great Eastern Railway 4-4-0 No. 1900 *Claud Hamilton*; built in 1900, its cab gives more protection than many of its contemporaries. The roof is white. (Author's collection)

81. London, Brighton & South Coast Railway 4-4-0 No. 43 *Duchess of Fife*, built 1902. (Author's collection)

82. A Midland Railway express leaves St Pancras hauled by 4-2-2 No. 672 and 4-4-0 No. 559. (Author's collection)

83. North British Railway 4-4-0 No. 884. (Author's collection)

84. The French-built De Glehn four-cylinder compound No. 102 *La France* was purchased by the GWR for comparative purposes, the English company supplying its tender. (Author's collection)

*Left:* 85. Poster advertising the Southern Belle. (Author's collection)

*Below:* 86. London, Brighton & South Coast railway 4-4-2 No. 40 heads the Southern Belle Pullman Car train. (Author's collection)

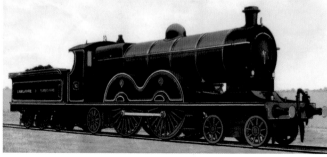

87. Lancashire & Yorkshire Railway 4-4-2 No. 1421 with 7-foot-3-inch-diameter driving wheels. (Author's collection)

88. North British British Railway 4-4-2 No. 868 *Aberdonian.* (Author's collection)

89. Caledonian Railway goods 4-6-0 No. 918. (Author's collection)

90. A Scotch express hauled by a London & North Western Railway 4-6-0 has a transport rival flying above. (Author's collection)

91. London & North Western Railway 4-6-0 *Experiment*. (Author's collection)

92. London, Brighton & South Coast Railway Terrier 0-6-0T No. 39 *Denmark*. Built in 1878, it was sold in 1902 to the contractor Messrs Pauling. (Author's collection)

93. Metropolitan Railway 0-6-4T No. 94 *Lord Aberconway*. (Author's collection)

94. Great Northern Railway 0-6-2T No. 190. (Author's collection)

95. North Staffordshire Railway 0-4-4T No. 9. (Author's collection)

96. A London & North Western Railway 4-4-2T over Bushey troughs. (Author's collection)

97. Midland Railway 0-6-4T No. 2000; these engines were nicknamed 'flat irons'. The gap in the side tank allowed the inside cylinders to be oiled. The class was prone to derailment. (Author's collection)

98. Hull & Barnsley Railway 0-6-2T No. 103. It carries a domeless boiler. (Author's collection)

99. Midland & Great Northern Railway 4-4-2T No. 41. (Author's collection)

100. A larger and more powerful goods locomotive could be made by adding a pony truck. GWR 2-6-0 No. 33 appeared in 1900. (Author's collection)

*Above left:* 101. Perth Central around 1910. (Author's collection)

*Below left:* 102. The 2.30 p.m. two-hour non-stop Birmingham express at Euston, headed by London & North Western Railway compound 4-4-0 No. 1973 *Hood*. (Author's collection)

*Bottom left:* 103. Cambrian Railways poster from around 1910. (Author's collection)

*Bottom right:* 104. Metropolitan Railway poster from around 1912. (Author's collection)

## Strike of Railwaymen and Others

The London & North Eastern Railway Co. wishes to notify their staff now on strike, that at the conclusion of the strike the number of staff whom the Company can employ will be materially reduced.

The effect of the strike upon the trade of the Country must be to diminish substantially the tonnage of traffic to be handled, and it will necessarily take a considerable time for trade to recover.

The Company wishes it to be understood that at the conclusion of the strike they will give preference for employment to those of their staff who have remained at work, or who offer themselves for re-employment without delay.

R. L. WEDGWOOD
CHIEF GENERAL MANAGER.

King's Cross Station London
12th May 1926.

LNER

*Above left:* 105. A 1912 GWR advertisement for one of its publications. (Author's collection)

*Above right:* 106. An advertisement for a Great Northern Railway bargain in 1910. (Author's collection)

*Right:* 107. An LNER poster issued on 12 May 1926 regarding the strike. (Author's collection)

108. An LMS poster publicising the Liverpool & Manchester Railway centenary celebrations. (Author's collection)

*Above left:* 109. A famous SR poster of 1936 based on a 1924 photograph of Waterloo station. (Author's collection)

*Above right:* 110. In 1935, the LNER publicised its new express service. (Author's collection)

*Above left:* 111. In 1937, the LMS announced its reply to the LNER. (Author's collection)

*Above right:* 112. An LNER poster of 1932. (Author's collection)

113. The LMS owned a modern hotel at Morecambe. (Author's collection)

## L·N·E·R CAMPING COACHES
### in England and Scotland
Accommodation for six persons from £2·10·0 per week
Ask for details at any L·N·E·R Station or Office

114. Who could resist renting an LNER camping coach in 1939? (Author's collection)

SOUTHERN RAILWAY

BOURNEMOUTH BELLE

ALL-PULLMAN EXPRESS – SUNDAYS until further notice
WATERLOO dep 10.30 BOURNEMOUTH C'L dep 6.20
SOUTHAMPTON WEST arr 11.59 SOUTHAMPTON WEST dep 7.0
BOURNEMOUTH C'L arr 12.39 WATERLOO arr 8.30
Cheap Return Fares from London to Southampton West 1st 20/-, 3rd 12/6
to Bournemouth C'L 1st 25/-, 3rd 15/- including Pullman Supplement

*Left:* 115. An SR poster of 1933. (Author's collection)

*Opposite, below:* 118. The Britannia Bridge over the Menai Strait around 1934. Damaged by fire in 1970, a road deck was added in 1980. (Author's collection)

*Right:* 116. A GWR poster advertising an air service from Birmingham to Cardiff, Haldon and Plymouth. (Author's collection)

*Above:* 117. An SR poster of 1936. (Author's collection)

THE BRITANNIA TUBULAR BRIDGE
MENAI STRAITS

*Above:* 119. An SR poster depicting Waterloo station in peacetime. (Author's collection)

*Left:* 120. A joint GWR and LMS poster for Weston-super-Mare issued in 1947. Although Weston-super-Mare was not on the LMS system, it ran through trains to this destination. (Author's collection)

three or four atmospheres. Next, a ring of masonry was erected. The two spans consisted of a wrought-iron oval tube forming an arch and two suspension chains, one on each side, connecting its two ends. It was thus a combination of arch and suspension construction. Each span – 455 feet in length, 56 feet in height and weighing 1,060 tons – was built on the Devonshire bank. They then had to be placed in position.

A span was placed on pontoons, floated into position and then, as the tide fell, rested on the piers, the lower girders only a few feet above the river. It was gradually raised by hydraulic jacks and the piers built up. The task took from 1 September 1857 to 19 May 1858. The eastern span was floated into position on 10 July 1858 and raised to its full height by December. The piers were of masonry except for the central one, which was stone up to about 12 feet above high water and above that comprised four octagonal cast-iron columns built up in sections.

John Anderson was the man behind the Callander & Oban Railway, becoming both secretary and manager. The project was beset with difficulties and did not reach its destination until 30 June 1880. The contractor was thoughtful, insulating the wooden huts with sawdust. It proved a valuable line for opening up connections with the Hebrides and for carrying fish and cattle. W. M. Acworth, in *The Railways of Scotland*, published in 1890, noted that steps had been taken to run fish trains after the signal boxes had closed for the night:

Arrangements have therefore been made by which the act of closing and locking the door of the booking office at intermediate stations diverts an electric current through a bell placed in the station master's bedroom, a current can therefore at any moment be sent along the line which will ring the bells and warn the station masters to get up and make the necessary arrangements for the coming train.

A particularly interesting stretch of line is where it runs on a ledge for 5 miles through the Pass of Brander. As boulders had fallen and derailed a passenger train, to avoid a recurrence a wire fence was erected connected to signals so that, in the event of a boulder breaking a wire, a signal would be thrown to danger. It was nicknamed 'Anderson's piano' because the wind whistling through the wires caused humming.

A line was also needed to serve Skye and this was the Dingwall & Skye Railway. Although its Act was passed in 1865, shareholders failed to pay the calls and the company was forced to terminate at Strome Ferry 10 miles short of the planned terminus at the Kyle of Lochalsh. The line opened to Strome Ferry on 19 August 1870 and eventually reached the Kyle of Lochalsh on 2 November 1897, by which time the company had been taken over by the Highland Railway.

The line was highly scenic, but severe gradients could cause steaming and adhesion problems. The rule book warned that 'all enginemen over the Skye line are hereby cautioned to keep a sharp lookout for signals from surface men who are watching for broken rails and dangers from swelling owing to intense frost'.

To help ease the two 2-4-0 locomotives round tight curves, the locomotive engineer, David Jones, proposed converting them to the 4-4-0 arrangement and they thus became known as 'Skye bogies'. They were prototypes for a class of bogie goods engines which were given smaller driving wheels. Around 1874 the Highland Railway owned about 420 miles of line, all of which was single track except for about half a dozen miles, and to work this great length of railway it had only sixty-seven engines.

A feature of Jones' engines was a curious chimney with louvres at the front. This chimney was double and the louvres were placed about midway up the outer casing. This was to counteract the effect of a high wind, which would check the draught on the fire. The air rising through the outer casing induced the necessary draught through the outer casing. To avoid igniting lineside vegetation, a spark arrester was fitted just below the foot of the chimney.

Jones' predecessor was William Stroudley, who introduced a bright yellow colour scheme with claret underframes. For about fifteen years, Jones continued this style.

Fort William was isolated for much of the nineteenth century, and to travel south to catch a train meant either a steamer to Oban or a coach to Kingussie, and neither was speedy. The West Highland Railway, backed by the North British, proposed to run from Craigendoran, cross Rannoch Moor and approach Fort William from the north.

Constructing the line across the almost virgin Rannoch Moor proved difficult, and when bankruptcy threatened to halt the project, a director, J. H. Renton, assisted financially and was rewarded by having his effigy displayed on a large granite slab at Rannoch station.

Construction was eased by a prefabricated steamer assembled on Loch Treig and used for carrying materials to the various sites. Many of the 4,000 men used in the construction were not the usual Irish navvies, but crofters and fishermen from the Hebrides. As there was no sleeping accommodation available locally, the contractors erected at intervals clusters of substantial and comfortable huts with good sleeping and cooking apartments. Where the crofters preferred to erect their own shelters of turf instead of lodging with strangers in the red-roofed huts of the company, the contractor helped to build them. The line opened between Helensburgh and Fort William on 7 August 1894.

It was felt desirable to lay an extension to the fishing port of Mallaig. As it was not really an economic proposition yet desirable from the social point of view, the Treasury took the highly unusual step of guaranteeing a minimum return of 3 per cent on a capital of £260,000, which was less than half the cost of the project. The North British guaranteed 3 per cent on half the difference between the actual cost and the government guarantee. (It actually took over the line on 31 December 1908.)

The contractor was Robert McAlpine – Concrete Bob – who rose from being a bricklayer's labourer to a small builder and then contractor. The West Highland company expected him to take five years or more to complete construction, yet he took only just over four years. He was one of the first to use concrete extensively and his bridge across Borrodale Burn had the world's largest concrete arch, of 127 feet, while the most important construction was Glenfinnan Viaduct, 416 yards in length, bearing twenty-one arches and set on a curve of 12 chains radius.

The workmen, termed 'McAlpine's Fusiliers', consisted largely of Lowland Scots and Irish with a smattering of Highlanders, fishermen from the Hebrides and Scandinavians. These navvies were no different from others and could suffer through drink, so police blockhouses were set up every 2 miles. W. H. Macpherson, in *Short Holidays in Small Open Boats*, wrote of a dispute between men from Ireland and those from Skye:

> But it was wonderful to see the tact and skill with which the police managed them. One sergeant, with his cane, in the midst of a half drunken, raging mob of navvies, threatening him with extermination was a fearsome sight! But one came to see by

degrees that they had in reality a great respect for him, and more or less recognized the fact of his authority.

The line opened on 1 April 1901 and made life in the area much pleasanter and easier. Before the coming of the railway, people in Mallaig needing to shop at Fort William had to walk 8 miles to Arisaig and then catch a coach which only ran three days a week for a return fare of £1 2s 0d for a journey of 34 miles taking seven and a half hours. The train did the whole journey from Mallaig to Fort William in an hour and three quarters and coal became cheaper than peat. The railway also allowed farmers and fishermen to get their produce to market in much better condition.

The end of the nineteenth century had two periods when there was a Race to the North. The first was in 1888, when the standard time for London to Edinburgh was ten hours from Euston via the West Coast route and nine from King's Cross via the East Coast. Then, on 2 June 1888, the London & North Western and the Caledonian, which operated the West Coast line, sped their service by an hour, making it equal their rivals. The East Coast retaliated on 18 July, cutting its time to eight and a half hours, while, from 1 August, the West Coast companies made the run in the same time. Not to be outdone, the East Coast introduced an eight-hour timing on 3 August, as did the West Coast on 6 August. Then, on 13 August, the hitherto rather staid North Eastern announced it would cut fifteen minutes from the schedule. The next day, the companies agreed on a minimum timing and racing ceased.

The opening of the Forth Bridge in 1890 allowed passengers between King's Cross and Aberdeen to travel in a through carriage as the Granton to Burntisland ferry was obviated. The

West Coast route Euston to Aberdeen was 539½ miles, but the East Coast route across the Forth Bridge only 523½ miles.

The Race to the North began seriously in 1895, when the East Coast route inaugurated a night express so that trains left Euston and King's Cross simultaneously at 8.00 p.m. The train from King's Cross was scheduled to arrive at Aberdeen at 7.20 a.m., that from Euston arriving twenty minutes later.

Drivers put it upon themselves to try and reach Aberdeen first. The railway authorities encouraged them by issuing faster timetables and not discouraging drivers from arriving early. Signalmen cleared their path by sidelining slower passenger and goods trains. Passengers at intermediate stations had to tolerate arriving at a station only to discover that the train they had intended to take had left before its booked time. This was not of much concern for those on the East Coast route, as a second Aberdeen train followed on the heels of the 8.00 p.m., but the West Coast route was forced to add a supplementary train. Speed restrictions were ignored as the trains sped through the night, buffeting their passengers in the process as the contemporary carriages did not give such a good ride as those we enjoy today.

The race really ended at Kinnaber Junction a few miles north of Montrose because the first past the junction was the winner, as the line onward to Aberdeen owned by the Caledonian Railway was used by both East and West Coast routes. At Kinnaber the signalman would gesture to a driver whether a rival was ahead or behind. Once there was a particularly exciting occasion when the signalman at Kinnaber Junction received simultaneously the bells for both competing trains. He chivalrously accepted the rival North British train.

In the third week of August, national newspapers started to report on each night's run. On the night of 20/21 August, the

West Coast train arrived at Kinnaber a minute ahead of the East Coast express. On the night of 21/22 August, a North British chief inspector travelled on the East Coast train from Edinburgh to Aberdeen and telegraphed to his general manager that he had crossed the Forth Bridge at 60 mph and the Tay Bridge at 52 mph – the speed restrictions were 40 mph and 25 mph respectively! The train had sped the 523½ miles in 520 minutes – an average speed of just over 60 mph. The North British general manager sensibly realised that far too many chances were being taken and that there was the grave risk of a tragedy, so put a stop to the racing. The following night, the West Coast route, not wishing to be beaten, covered their 540 miles in an astonishing 512 minutes.

On one occasion, the race train arrived at Aberdeen with seven passengers and the relief train with just one. Between 19 and 21 August 1895, the East Coast race trains carried 101 passengers and their opponents thirty-five. It is interesting to contemplate what the passengers did when they arrived at Aberdeen about 4.30 a.m.

The race was not an economic success. The East Coast route carried more passengers than the West when the races began, and at the end of the contest this fact was still true. The companies agreed to end racing and agreed on an East Coast timing of 10 hours 25 minutes and the West Coast with a 16½ mile longer journey should take 10 hours 30 minutes. This meant that speeds hardly increased over subsequent years and it was said that dead fish travelled from Aberdeen to London faster than live passengers.

Similar competition took place on the Great Western and London & North Western routes for London to Birmingham; the London & North Western and Midland routes for London to Manchester; and the Great Western and the London & South Western routes for Plymouth to London.

But what was happening elsewhere in the country? At the same time as the Race to the North, there was a long correspondence in *The Times* in September 1895 under the heading 'The Crawl to the South'. One so-called express to Hastings was described by an unfortunate passenger:

It was a light train running on a lovely afternoon, and there was no snow or rain, no head wind or fog. We swept on so rapidly that the speed could not alarm the most timid. We did not scamp a single stoppage, and yet we steamed into Victoria at 5.30 so proudly that I felt sure we must have arrived unexpectedly early. The time-table (a work of fiction!) indeed, made us arrive at 4.37, but this I saw must be merely a printer's error. Is there another line in the world that would dare to run such a train at the break-neck speed of 74 miles in 200 minutes?

Not for nothing was the London, Brighton & South Coast Railway nicknamed the 'Brighton and Slow Coach Railway'. *The Times* editorial wrote,

The Southern managers have no doubt been aware that it would be of very little use for them to attempt to rival the magnificent performances of the Great Northern and London and North-Western companies. Their rolling stock and the well-established traditions of their companies put it out of the question that they should try this with success. They have hit accordingly upon another method of distinguishing themselves more suited to their capacities. They have chosen frankly a very different form of distinction, and the struggle between them now is which of them can claim to have established the slowest, the most unpunctual, and the most inconvenient service of trains.

The Great Western also had an inconvenience – that of the broad gauge preventing through running to the lines of other companies. The problem had to be solved, so, on Friday 20 May 1892, the last broad gauge train left Paddington. As it returned, each station master certified that no broad gauge rolling stock remained in his sidings. At Swindon, 13 miles of temporary sidings were laid to accommodate the redundant broad gauge stock. So efficient was the work of conversion that a standard gauge train was able to run on the evening of 21 May from Exeter to Plymouth, and the regular service resumed over the former broad gauge lines on Monday 23 May. For the task of conversion, permanent way employees were assisted by approximately 3,400 other railwaymen and all were presented by W. H. Wills, a GWR director and also chairman of the tobacco firm, with 5,000 2 oz packets of Westward Ho!.

After the opening in 1899 of the Great Central Railway from the Midlands to Marylebone, no major lines were built in Britain apart from the GWR's cut-offs. By the end of the Victorian era, longer rails, less joints and bogie stock gave passengers a more comfortable ride.

James Holden of the Great Eastern Railway built the first oil-fired British locomotive in 1893, the 2-4-0 *Petrolia*. He used the gas-oil residue which remained following the production of gas for carriage lighting. Steam was initially raised by coal, and then oil took over. Oil flowed on to an open-ended tray designed so that the oil spread evenly over the surface before flowing over the open edge of the tray in the form of a fine film or ribbon. As it fell, it was broken into very minute particles by steam or compressed air.

The weight of the oil required was from one-half to two-thirds that of coal, and savings in labour were effected at engine depots as the oil was supplied by pumps and there were no ashes or clinker to dispose of, and boiler tubes did not become clogged, thus giving a locomotive much greater availability.

Coal was cheaper than oil in Britain, so the latter was only used during strikes that restricted coal supplies, which occurred in 1912, 1921 and 1926. In 1945, when there was a shortage of good steam coal because the best was exported to obtain foreign currency, the GWR equipped some engines for oil firing. When drawing a heavy load, an oil-fired 2-8-0 burned 6.5 gallons per mile, compared with 72 lb of coal, which meant that the range of an oil-fired engine was approximately half as much again as one using coal.

The Ministry of Transport thought it an excellent scheme and authorised other main-line companies to convert 1,217 engines from coal to oil firing. Then, after many locomotives had been converted and money invested on oil fuelling plants, the Treasury announced that there was not enough foreign exchange available to purchase the oil!

# 8

# Narrow Gauge, Industrial and Light Railways

Although the standard gauge of 4 foot 8½ inches was suitable for the majority of railways in Britain, in certain conditions a narrow gauge could be advantageous – less land was required, and curves could be tighter and thus follow the contours more easily and require fewer earthworks. The Ffestiniog Railway disproved the theory that narrow gauge locomotives and rolling stock would be dangerously top-heavy; in fact, locomotives and stock of standard gauge dimensions could be used on 3 foot gauge track, and in difficult terrain either the 3 foot, the metre, or the 3 foot 6 inch gauge was adopted. Although popular in developing countries, these gauges were only used in the British Isles on the Isle of Man and in remote parts of Ireland. Narrow gauge railways generally have a combined buffer and coupling, rather than these forming separate items.

The Ffestiniog Railway was the first of the longer-distance narrow gauge railways. With a gauge of only 1 feet 11½ inches it opened in 1836. It was chiefly laid on a falling gradient of 1 in 80 to allow working by gravity, horses drawing empty wagons the 13 miles from Portmadoc to Blaenau Ffestiniog. Steam locomotives were introduced on the line in 1863, and two years later it became a public railway, carrying passengers and general goods.

The year 1869 saw the appearance of the Fairlie locomotive. Designed by Robert Francis Fairlie, who was trained on the London & North Western, in 1864 he patented a double-ended locomotive with two boilers and a central cab. It was mounted on two powered bogies. It proved very successful, as the bogies distributed the weight over a greater length than a normal engine and also eased it round curves rather than forcing the wheels into a curve as happened with a conventional fixed-wheelbase machine. His concept proved a success and similar railways opened in different parts of the world.

Following the success of his narrow gauge locomotive, he designed the 0-4-4T standard gauge engine used on the Swindon, Marlborough & Andover Railway. At first glance it appeared to be a normal engine, but closer inspection revealed that the driving wheels were not fixed to the frames, but on a bogie. It was also one of the first engines in Britain to be fitted with Walschaert's valve gear. This single-boiler Fairlie had the advantage of greater tractive effort than a conventional engine of the same weight and cylinder capacity, because having its driving wheels on a bogie reduced friction as curves could be negotiated more easily.

The flexible steam pipe between the boiler and bogie constantly failed and coal consumption was heavy – possibly because the locomotive foreman at Swindon did not fully understand the valve gear. Nicknamed 'Jumbo', she was kept for reserve use and was certainly a white elephant. A similar engine used on the Great Southern & Western Railway in Ireland proved very satisfactory and had a coal consumption of 3–4 lbs per mile less than average. In 1871, the Ffestiniog Railway achieved another first – bogie coaches set on iron frames.

Perhaps rather surprisingly in view of the fact that narrow gauge railways were particularly suitable for mountainous regions, Scotland had only one narrow gauge passenger railway. This was the Campbeltown & Machrihanish Railway, which opened as recently as 1906 and carried passengers for 6½ miles across the Kintyre peninsula from Campbeltown to the Atlantic coast. The line had started life in 1876 as a 2 foot 3 inch gauge line between Kilkivan colliery and Campbeltown. When the pit became exhausted in 1881, a line was laid to the new Argyle colliery, closer to Machrihanish, and this line when extended became the light railway. The introduction of a turbine steamer in 1901 saw an extension of tourist traffic from the Clyde to Campbeltown, where tourists wished to cross the peninsula to visit the Atlantic coast. The light railway fulfilled the demand to satisfy this need. It had six intermediate halts.

The colliery closed in 1929, and by then serious competition had arisen from two bus companies and the line closed entirely in November 1931. When the colliery reopened in 1945, road transport was considered more economic.

Until 1874, the 1 foot 11½ inch gauge was the narrowest in use, but then an engineer, Sir Arthur Heywood of Duffield Bank, near Derby, built a 15 inch gauge line to serve his estate, a railway being a neater and cheaper way of handling a small flow of traffic. To cope with tight curves, his home-built six- and eight-wheeled coupled locomotives had a flexible wheelbase.

His idea did not generally catch on, only the Duke of Westminster commissioning a similar line for his estate at Eaton Hall, near Chester; horse and cart, or later the motor lorry, proved cheaper and more flexible.

# Industrial Railways

The first railways were industrial lines, and then, as the large public railways developed, factories, mines and quarries were served either by sidings or an independent line taking wagons to and from exchange sidings. Many heavy industries made use of railways: brickworks, docks, electricity and gas works, military camps, oil refineries, quarries, sewage works, steelworks and waterworks. Breweries at Burton-on-Trent ran an extensive network of lines and also distilleries, especially on Speyside. Some industrial railways were of considerable size and extent, with many miles of track and a large locomotive stud.

Wagon movement might be by steam engine, horse power, gravity, cable haulage from a capstan turned by hydraulic or electrical power, a stationary engine with a cable or even just manpower, perhaps aided by a pinch bar – a long wooden pole with a metal end placed under a wheel and used to lever it along.

One fascinating engineless method of working an industrial railway was a balanced incline, whereby a descending loaded wagon had a cable at its tail which ran to the top of the incline and traversed a wheel which could be braked, the cable then descending to an empty wagon at the foot of the incline, requiring it to be drawn up. Gravity did all the work gratis. For economy, the track was often not double throughout, rather being single at the top and bottom with a central passing loop. Where traffic did not allow such an economic method of working, a stationary engine could be used to draw up wagons. The last standard gauge, cable-worked incline in commercial use was at Whitehaven and stopped working in 1986.

Industrial lines often used second-hand main-line locomotives in the early days, but, as these grew in size and industrial lines were often laid with lightweight rails with sharp curves, the increasing size of ex-main-line locomotives made them unsuitable. Some engine builders, such as Hunslet, Manning, Wardle, and Peckett, specialised in producing industrial locomotives, generally 0-4-0STs or 0-6-0STs. Although industrial railways were early users of locomotives with internal combustion engines, steam traction remained on industrial railways in Britain until the 1980s, long after the end of steam on BR in 1968.

Most private sidings were built to the standard gauge, but others, if merely for internal use or for providing transfer traffic to a main line, could be narrow gauge; for example, the London & North Western at its Crewe works and the railway at Woolwich Arsenal used a 1 foot 6 inch gauge.

In 1877, Paul Décauville started producing all-metal prefabricated track in various gauges. This could be laid Hornby-style and easily moved to a different location when needed. It was particularly used when a line was only required for a brief time – such as a road or railway construction project or when creating a large housing estate, harbour breakwater or reservoir. It also proved valuable in the First World War, serving the trenches.

# Light Railways

An ordinary railway built under an Act of Parliament was required to provide for passengers the following: a station, platform, waiting room, toilet, clock, signals and, if it had a level crossing, someone to work the gates. These things were admirable and acceptable on a profitable line and their expense could be taken from revenue. As the nineteenth century wore on, there were a few rural areas not served by a railway and where one would be desirable, but where the revenue would be just insufficient to pay for these things. A cheaper kind of railway was required, yet one which was still safe for public use.

The Railway Construction Facilities Act of 1864 permitted a line to be built without the need for an Act if all the landowners on the route agreed to sell the land required by the railway. This facility avoided considerable legal expenses in obtaining an Act. A light railway could be constructed at a cost of about £3,000 a mile, approximately a quarter the cost of a normal branch line.

The Railway Regulation Act of 1868 specified a 'light railway' as having an axle load restricted to 8 tons and speed to 25 mph. This led to the Light Railways Act of 1896, which facilitated the construction of minor railways. Its main provisions were:

1. It set up a Light Railway Commission of three members to consider each proposed line.
2. Instead of having to obtain an Act of Parliament and having to pay the associated legal costs, these commissioners, subject to the Board of Trade's approval, could grant a Light Railway Order.
3. In addition to the public subscribing, local authorities could also contribute, or make loans. Where money was advanced, a Treasury loan of 25 per cent was also available.
4. The Treasury could grant loans of up to 50 per cent of the capital cost if the Board of Agriculture certified that a light railway was necessary to develop a district.
5. The commissioners and the Board of Trade were granted powers which allowed them to relax the need for some provisions, e.g. platforms were not essential; if coaches were suitably adapted, access could be from ground level; platforms were not required to be staffed; an ungated level crossing

could be protected by having trains approach at a limit of 5 mph. Animals could be prevented from straying along the track by a cattle grid – a set of knife-edge vertical boards. Signalling could be simplified.

6. A Light Railway Order would authorise compulsory land purchase, owners' compensation taking account of the benefits the railway would bring.

7. Existing railways could apply for an order and be converted to a light railway.

Between 1898 and 1918, 687 applications were made for Light Railway Orders. Only 900 miles were actually built and 350 miles of these were street tramways.

Main-line railways promoted light railways and sometimes took over independent lines. The Kelvedon, Tiptree & Tollesbury Light Railway (one of its coaches appeared in the film *The Titfield Thunderbolt*) was worked by the Great Eastern, while the Cambrian Railways worked, or owned, several light railways. In the 1923 Grouping, some light railways were taken over by one of the Big Four – the Cleobury Mortimer & Ditton Priors Light Railway coming under the Great Western umbrella.

The timing of the Light Railways Act was unfortunate because by the time the lines had been built and were starting to pay for the investment made in them, they were facing serious road competition.

Col. H. E Stephens ran thirteen light railways from his office at Tonbridge. An innovation as early as 1921 was the purchase of a petrol-driven railcar for the shuttle service between Clevedon and Weston-super-Mare, this taking place in the same year that he used a converted farm tractor for shunting on a lightly laid wharf line on the Weston, Clevedon & Portishead Light

Railway. In the winter, Stephens employed otherwise redundant staff manufacturing concrete sleeper blocks. Sebastian Meyer was another collector of light railways, owning eight in eastern England, and at the Grouping in 1923 most were absorbed into other lines.

Only three independent light railways were nationalised in 1948: the East Kent, the Kent & East Sussex and the Shropshire & Montgomeryshire. The final independent light railway, the Derwent Valley in Yorkshire, closed in 1988.

The Kent & East Sussex has been reopened by volunteers; indeed, Light Railway Orders are used by preservation societies to achieve authority to operate their lines.

The term 'light railway' is used for the Docklands Light Railway in London and for the Light Rapid Transit systems set up in some British cities over the last thirty years. Although their purpose is different, they still use the principle of lightweight track, structures and rolling stock.

# 9

# The Heyday of the Steam Railway, 1900–1914: the Rise and Fall of the Steam Rail Motor

The beginning of the twentieth century was the golden age for steam traction. The Midland had dispensed with second class from 1 January 1875, other companies following suit from 1885. This move offered the public second-class accommodation at third-class fares, though from 1956 British Railways referred to third class as second class. Coaches were improved towards the close of the nineteenth century and, instead of running on four or six wheels, were placed on four- or six-wheeled bogies, giving a superior ride. Lighting was by oil, gas or electricity, while steam heating replaced foot warmers. A clerestory roof improved ventilation and lighting.

The Midland was the first to offer upholstered, instead of wooden, seats to third-class passengers. Its coaches were comfortable, relatively spacious and had toilet facilities. On long journeys, restaurant and sleeping cars were provided. Above all, railways held a monopoly of land transport: there might be a rival railway, but there was no competing road or air service.

Longer-distance trains had dining and sleeping cars, which could be reached by corridors. The Great Western produced the first through corridor train in 1891, which offered greater comfort when travelling long distances as lavatories could be provided. (For those interested, footplatemen used a bucket which was rinsed out at the end of a turn and then used for washing so that they could go home clean.) Sensitively, men's and women's lavatories were separate and at opposite ends of the carriages. Unlike later corridor coaches, the flexible bellows between coaches were offset rather than placed centrally, which meant that the train had to remain as a block set. The corridors were intended simply to offer lavatory access and the gangway connections were locked to prevent third-class passengers sneaking into first-class accommodation.

Some companies, such as the Caledonian, Cambrian and North British, anxious that their new lavatory carriages should seat the same number of passengers per compartment as their predecessors, padded the lavatory doors and placed hinged seats in front of them. What delicate and sensitive Victorian ladies thought of this arrangement can only be imagined!

These improvements added to the weight of trains, as corridors meant the sacrifice of two seats in every compartment while a dining car replaced a coach of fare-paying passengers. The weight of express trains rose from approximately 100 tons to 250 tons, so locomotives had to be more powerful. A six-wheeled coach weighed about 15 tons, whereas a side-corridor coach was 30 tons; the weight of twelve-wheel dining and sleeping cars could be 40 tons or more.

A West Coast Scotch express of 1893 weighed 252 tons empty and accommodated less than 200 passengers, so for every passenger in a full train 1¼ tons had to be hauled by the locomotive. This contrasted strongly with Great Western second-class coaches of the 1840s, in which ten people were carried for every ton of dead weight. In the Edwardian period, when most companies' coaches were 60 feet in length, the GWR built 68–70-foot coaches weighing only 33 tons and seating eighty third-class passengers; so being able to carry 2.4 passengers per ton of dead weight in a corridor coach was excellent.

In the post-Grouping era, the LMS and LNER standardised on third-class passengers being accommodated in compartments of three a side with armrests, whereas the GWR and SR had four on each side and no arm rests. Interestingly, in BR days this continued: it built two versions of the same stock, one with three a side for the northern lines and another with four a side for the southern.

Although most companies had gone over to bogie coaches by the start of the twentieth century, the North London Railway never owned a vehicle with more than four wheels and was constructing such coaches for the Broad Street to Richmond line as late as 1910. They lasted, though not on that route, until the beginning of the Second World War.

Foot warmers, initially hot water but later filled with sodium acetate, were replaced by steam heating, though the SR's Barnstaple to Lynton narrow gauge line used foot warmers until 1933. The Midland Railway's Pullman coaches had a circuit of hot-water pipes heated by an oil-fired boiler, while in the late eighties the Caledonian used exhaust steam from the Westinghouse brake pump to heat coaches. The Glasgow & South Western had an ingenious system costing nothing. Above the flame of the compartment oil lamp was a small boiler with pipes leading to a heater below a seat. If the lamp was unlit, passengers stayed cold.

In the 1880s, oil gas gradually replaced oil lamps. The gas was carried in cylinders holding a forty-hour supply and used fishtail, or, in the better stock, Argand annular burners. Electric lighting began to replace gas lighting and, although a little brighter than gas, offered a less steady light, while the carbon-filament lamps were fragile and unreliable. Change to electricity was therefore slow, despite the fact that gas caused some accidents to become immeasurably worse. For instance, on 22 May 1915, due to signalmen's errors, a troop train collided head-on with a local passenger train at Quintinshill and into this wreckage piled the Scotch express. The troop train was gas lit, and just before leaving the gas cylinders had been fully charged to a pressure of from five to six atmospheres. Coal from the overturned engine of the troop train ignited this gas and created an inferno. Water was taken from the tanks of two nearby goods engines and a pump and hose connected to a stream at a neighbouring farm. All that day and through the following night, the holocaust continued. Eight passengers were killed in the express, two in the stopping train and probably 215 in the troop train, but the exact number could never be established. In addition, two railway servants were killed.

Electric lighting on trains at first used batteries, an example of this being on the London, Brighton & South Coast Railway. The Midland Railway's electric lights were initially dim, particularly when a train was halted and insufficient light prevented reading. The Midland tried electric lighting in their Pullmans, but found gas better.

The London & North Western Ramsbottom 7 foot 6 inch, single-driver No. 44, *Harlequin*, built in February 1860, was equipped with a steam-driven dynamo on the tender. Its attendant was in a dangerous position up high, and had to beware of striking his head on an overhead bridge. Each compartment had two lamps and an automatic switch ensured that if one failed, the other would come on. It offered a better light than other systems, but only worked if an engine was on a train. It was only suitable for a fixed train set, as only some of the company's coaches were equipped for electric lighting.

An improvement in 1894 was for each coach to have its own generating plant. With the first scheme the output of most axle-driven dynamos varied with the train's speed, but with J. Stone & Company's system, after a predetermined limit, the dynamo speed was constant, thus putting less wear and tear on the system. On 27 November 1895, the London, Tilbury & Southend Railway was the first to adopt Stone's system. It had double batteries to offer flicker-free lighting. The lights were controlled from the guard's van. The running cost of Stone's system was just that of fuel, one-twentieth lb of coal per coach per mile.

| | |
|---|---|
| Annual cost of oil lighting | 0.075*d* per candle power per hour excluding interest of capital outlay |
| Annual cost of Stone's lighting | 0.006*d* per candle power per hour excluding interest on capital outlay |

Stone's system cost only one-eighth of the cost of oil gas, including the capital outlay, and saved the employees work and avoided inconvenience to passengers.

Labour was plentiful and relatively cheap, and arguably it was during this era that Britain's locomotive liveries were at their finest. The large Edwardian engines had a considerable space on which to display their finery.

The most common colour was green, varying from the light apple green of the Great Northern to the darker green of the

Great Western. But they were not just a plain colour all over – lining was employed to bring out their beauty. Great Northern engines had black bands around the boiler and a white line each side of the black, while the underframe was painted maroon, lined red. The engine number and letters 'GNR' were in yellow, shaded with red.

GWR engines were lined in black and orange. The splashers, frames and wheels were a deep Indian red. The tender bore an elaborate monogram of the letters 'GWR' in gold, relieved and shaded in black and burnt sienna. The name and number plates were of polished brass, this metal also being used tastefully as decoration elsewhere.

Midland engines of the period were painted a dark red banded with a black line which had a yellow stripe each side. The cab interior was painted light oak edged with black. Buffer beams were vermillion, carrying the letters 'MR' in gold, shaded with blue, a similar device appearing on the tender. Engine numbers were in brass, though from 1906 they were replaced by very large numbers on the tender. This practice, also used by the Southern in its early days, had the disadvantage that if a tender became faulty and needed exchanging, it displayed an incorrect number.

There was one instance where this occurred and paper had been stuck over the incorrect number and the new number painted on. Unfortunately, rain and wind caused some of the paper to blow off and different numbers, neither correct, were displayed on both sides of the tender.

Both the Caledonian and the Somerset & Dorset Joint Railway favoured blue, the former using a light shade and the latter a darker. Somerset & Dorset engines were lined in black with yellow on each side. The vermillion buffer beams were lined. Great Eastern engines bore a similar livery.

In chief mechanical engineer Stroudley's time, London, Brighton & South Coast engines wore a startling yellow ochre livery with a border of dark olive edged with a black band. Frames were claret with black edging. The brass number plates bore a bright blue ground, while the locomotive's name was in gold with bluish-green shading; the coupling rods were claret. The cab interior was a stone colour with the driver's name in block capitals between the windows. A driver kept to his own engine, which had the advantage that he cared for it – this perhaps offsetting the economy which could have been made had it been placed in general use.

In 1905, Marsh, who had succeeded Stroudley, modified the LB&SCR livery to reduce the painting costs. Passenger locomotives were umber, express engines lined with two gold lines, while tank engines had two red lines. The cab interiors remained light stone.

Until 1907, London, Tilbury & Southend engines were light green, but that year an unusual lavender-grey livery appeared. It did not wear well, and in 1910 the pre-1907 livery returned.

Many railways used an economical black livery for their goods locomotives, but the London & North Western also used it for their passenger engines, lining them with a light-blue line spanned on each side with a fine white line and a vermillion line set at a 1½-inch distance. Number plates were brass with polished brass figures on a red background. To celebrate Queen Victoria's Jubilee in 1897, *Great Britain* was painted poppy red while *Queen Empress* appeared in white with gilt lettering.

The invention of the transfer by Tearnes in 1856 was a great timesaver when applying numerals, lettering and coasts of arms.

A network of lines covered Britain and it was only the most remote areas with a very low population that were not served by a railway. Almost every village and town of importance had its own station, and sometime had more than one. For example, Barnstaple, with a population of about 10,000, enjoyed no less than three: the GWR station, the London & South Western's Barnstaple Junction and Barnstaple Town, the latter also shared with the narrow gauge Lynton & Barnstaple Railway.

Almost all goods sold in shops arrived at the nearest railway station and were delivered by the railway company itself, or an associated carrier. Groceries, ironmongery, haberdashery, beer, books, builders' supplies and London newspapers all arrived by rail, as did the post.

Passenger trains could be classified into two types: express and stopping passenger, the latter also including branch trains. Goods trains might be specialised, perhaps carrying solely coal, iron ore or oil, while others would have wagons carrying various loads. Perishable traffic needed fast delivery, sometimes by express freight, or as 'tail traffic' hanging on the rear of a passenger train. Bacon products from such firms as Messrs Harris, Calne, travelled in this manner. Soft fruit from Hampshire, the Cheddar Valley or the Vale of Evesham also needed to reach its destination quickly. Early potatoes from the Channel Islands arrived at Weymouth quay by GWR steamer and were transferred to rail for onward delivery. In 1908, as many as 300 wagons were dealt with daily at Weymouth, and, due to the short shelf life of flowers, new potatoes, tomatoes, broccoli and other vegetables from France, rapid transport was essential.

Milk was another important traffic, and many rural stations despatched churns to the large cities, the churns being returned empty. In 1902, 2.5 million gallons of milk were consumed weekly and the Thames at Teddington Weir could flow for two hours with the equivalent of milk consumed in London over a year. Some 40,000 wagons of eggs were carried on British railways annually, and if put in a line these vans would have stretched 150 miles from Paddington to Bridgwater. If all the cheese carried by British railways annually was made into one large cheese, it would have filled Westminster Abbey. The general charge railways made for carrying 56 lb a distance of 100 miles was 1s 9d, while the Great Eastern charged a very reasonable 4d for 20 lb from any station on its line to Liverpool Street.

The trend continued, larger locomotives being built to haul the ever-heavier passenger trains. Many railways favoured a 4-2-2 for fast passenger trains, but increasingly heavier trains began to defeat them. H. A. Ivatt's Great Northern answer was Britain's first 4-4-2, which allowed a longer boiler while the rear pony track offered space for a wider firebox. A better solution and one which offered a better footing was Wilson Worsdell's first British 4-6-0, which appeared in 1899.

When an engine starts, it tends to come back on to its rear wheels, and if these are coupled then adhesion is improved. In 1903, the Caledonian Railway's J. F. McIntosh built two 4-6-0s which he claimed were Britain's largest and most powerful express engines. They were intended for the Carlisle to Glasgow route with its Beattock Bank of 10 miles of 1 in 75. He brought out a larger version in 1906, the Cardean class 4-6-0, *Cardean* herself working almost daily the 2.00 p.m. from Glasgow to Euston on its first leg to Carlisle. It returned with the corresponding Down train. When *Cardean* was tested on the London & North Western route over Shap Fell, she maintained a speed of 44 mph up the 1 in 125 gradient.

In 1898, Wilhelm Schmitt developed the superheater. Steam produced in a boiler is saturated steam and contains water. It cools when it comes into contact with pipes and cylinders, and water droplets are formed that resist the movement of the pistons. If extra heat is given to saturated steam, its moisture content is changed to additional steam and it becomes a gas and thus eliminates power loss due to condensation. Steam also expands as it absorbs this extra heat and so more power can be produced. Superheating increases a locomotive's power by up to 25 per cent.

In 1899, George Hughes of the Lancashire & Yorkshire Railway was the first in Britain to use a superheater, followed by George Churchward of the GWR, while in 1914 Henry Fowler found that a superheated Midland compound showed a saving in coal and water consumption.

The Swindon superheater proved highly successful and almost all subsequent GWR locomotives, apart from shunting engines, were fitted with one. It saved approximately 15 per cent of coal.

The Sunny South Express was worked by the London & North Western from Rugby to Willdesden Junction where a London, Brighton & South Coast engine took it on to Brighton. The LB&SCR had their I3 class 4-4-2Ts fitted with Schmitt superheaters. In 1909, it was decided to run one engine throughout. LB&SCR No. 23 worked from Brighton to Rugby and returned the next day, while LNWR 4-4-0 Precursor class No. 7 *Titan*, using only saturated steam, made corresponding workings on the same two days.

The last water stop going north was at East Croydon, 90½ miles from Rugby, and the 4-4-2T had no provision for picking up water from the LNWR troughs. The engine managed the journey and burnt only 27 lb of coal per mile, a 3¼-ton bunker of coal lasting from Brighton back to Brighton. Its tank capacity was 2,110 gallons. The trials lasted a month and No. 23 was occasionally relieved by No. 26 of the same class. C. J.

Bowen-Cooke was impressed by this performance and introduced superheaters in 1910 on his 4-4-0 George the Fifth class and in 1911 his Prince of Wales class.

A locomotive trial took place between a GWR Star class 4-6-0 and a LNWR Experiment class with the same wheel arrangement. It occurred because the GWR chief mechanical engineer, George Jackson Churchward, was asked by his board why the LNWR could build three 4-6-0s for the cost of two on the GWR, to which he retorted, 'Because one of mine could pull two of their b— things backwards!'

It was at the height of the August holidays and, wishing to keep the best for their own use, Camden sent *Worcestershire*, their worst Experiment class engine. Hauling the heavy west of England expresses, she lost a lot of time and extra water stops had to be made. On Up trips she was piloted from Exeter to Savernake and on the last down journey she failed at Exeter, whereas the GWR Stars had handled these trains faultlessly and economically.

In 1901, Churchward set out a range of standard classes on the GWR which proved suitable for the next fifty years. The first, No. 100, *William Dean*, was almost entirely different from any other previous GWR engine. In addition to having six-coupled wheels, it had inside frames and outside cylinders, whereas most of its predecessors had outside frames and inside cylinders. The cylinders had the longest stroke the company had ever used and piston – not slide – valves were fitted. In 1903, it was given a 200 lb tapered boiler and became a member of the 4-6-0 Saint class. The taper boiler was better than the parallel pattern as it improved water circulation, giving more even steam production.

Churchward knew that the de Glehn compound 4-4-2s were doing excellent work in France, proving to be fast, economical machines. He took the highly unusual step of persuading his directors to purchase one in order to compare them with his own machines. To make the comparison fairer, he converted one of his 4-6-os to a 4-4-2. Little difference was found in the coal consumption of the English and French engines and more oil was used on the mechanically more complicated French engine. The purchase was not a waste of money, as Churchward improved his bogies by replacing the swing link with a side control spring as on the French locomotive. He also built the Star class, a four-cylinder version of his 4-6-0.

Churchward constructed the first British 2-8-0 goods engine in 1903 and this design was perpetuated until the last was built in 1942. Many of the other railway companies were still building 0-6-os for freight work, but the introduction of express goods trains in the twentieth century required running at 50–60 mph and thus a more powerful and stable machine than a 0-6-0, so, in 1911–12, 2-6-os were produced by Churchward on the Great Western and Gresley on the Great Northern.

An important development in 1906 on the Great Western Railway, regrettably not copied by other railways until about fifty years later, was the Automatic Train Control. This consisted of a ramp laid between the rails near a distant signal. If that signal stood at clear, the ramp was electrified and, through a shoe on a locomotive, rang a bell in the engine's cab. If the signal was at Caution, or the apparatus had failed, the ramp remained electrically dead and caused a steam whistle to sound in the cab until silenced by the driver. It proved invaluable, especially in fog. The system was improved even further when a Caution signal also opened a valve admitting air to the vacuum pipe and thus applied the brakes on both engine and train.

Many late nineteenth-century locomotives had inside cylinders, a situation where they were kept warm and less likely to impart a twisting movement to the frames. This type of engine necessarily required a crank axle, and the larger engines, being built with increased power, severely stressed the cranks and increased maintenance costs. To avoid this problem, many British railways reverted to outside cylinders. Some railways favoured three- or four-cylinder engines, the first three-cylinder engine being Holden's 0-10-0T referred to below. Raven of the North Eastern and Gresley of the Great Northern also favoured three-cylinder locomotives. Two-cylinder engines were generally preferred for everything except the heaviest passenger trains, and many drivers considered a two-cylinder engine better for hard slogging but a four-cylinder for offering a better ride at high speed.

In 1908, the very first 4-6-2 in Britain was built at Swindon. Named *The Great Bear*, she was built for prestige rather than for necessity and was something of a white elephant. Her weight and length restricted her to the Paddington to Bristol run, though very occasionally she was spotted elsewhere. Another problem was that the inside axle boxes of the pony truck tended to run hot due to the close proximity of the ash pan. The Great Western never built another Pacific, finding 4-6-0s quite adequate for its needs, though the Great Northern, and later the LMS, LNER and SR, made use of this wheel arrangement.

Some British locomotive engineers ignored the work of Churchward and simply built larger versions of earlier designs; thus Drummond's Paddleboxes, Hughes' Lancashire & Yorkshire four-cylinder 4-6-0s and the Great Central's Sir Sam Fay class looked impressive, yet actually performed little better than a 4-4-0.

Although compounding generally failed to find favour in Britain, W. M. Smith's design on the North Eastern Railway inspired the

Midland Railway's S. W. Johnson to build a compound 4-4-0 using Smith's system. Found satisfactory, his successor, W. M. Deeley, added to the class. Tests run by the LMS in 1924 to 1925 revealed that Midland compounds with a large cylinder, which used second-hand steam from two smaller cylinders, offered greater fuel economy than larger, simple-expansion 4-6-0s, so initially this design was chosen to be a standard LMS type. In the Smith and Smith-Deeley compounds the engine could be worked as simple, semi-compound or full compound.

To start a Deeley compound, a driver opened the regulator to about 20 degrees of the handle quadrant to admit high-pressure steam to all three cylinders: to the low-pressure cylinder through an extra port, and through a small port to the high-pressure cylinders. When the regulator was opened wider, the main high-pressure ports were opened while the port to the low-pressure cylinder was closed and the engine went over to compound working. It could be worked semi-compound by closing the regulator while at speed and then reopening to the starting position, which allowed a limited amount of auxiliary high-pressure steam to be admitted to the low-pressure steam chest.

At the start of the twentieth century, electric power was rearing its head. In 1901, a planned competitive electric railway threatened the Great Eastern's income in north-east London. The great advantage of electric traction, its backers proclaimed, was that it could accelerate from a standstill to 30 mph in thirty seconds.

James Holden of the Great Eastern, not to be outdone, built a three-cylinder 0-10-0T which could accelerate to 30 mph in thirty seconds with a 335-ton train. Although it was a success and defeated the electric scheme, the engine was too heavy for much of the Great Eastern track and was converted to a 0-8-0 tender engine.

In the same period, electric tramways were being introduced into many British towns and cities and competed with short-distance rail passenger traffic. Some railways contested by also electrifying, as did the London, Brighton & South Coast Railway in 1909 and the London & North Western in 1914, while as early as 1903 and 1904 the Mersey Railway and the Lancashire & Yorkshire Railway had electrified their lines in the Liverpool area, as did the North Eastern its Teeside lines in 1904.

Other railways used the steam rail motor as the answer. Basically, it was a coach with a steam engine built into one end. Capable of being driven from either end, it obviated the time and trouble needed to run a conventional locomotive round to the other end of its train when reaching a terminus. The fireman, of course, stayed in the cab of the rail motor.

The first design, by Drummond of the London & South Western, appeared in 1903 on the Fratton to East Southsea branch, jointly owned with the London, Brighton & South Coast Railway. It commenced regular working on 1 June 1903 and operated a twenty-minute-interval service. It lacked the ability to raise sufficient steam and for rush-hour services had to have a steam locomotive attached, this completely cancelling out any saving. When its boiler was replaced with one of a larger pattern, it could work unaided. Interestingly, the locomotive section was painted in LSWR green and the coach section in LB&SCR livery of chocolate and cream.

Meanwhile, an American sought powers to construct a network of electric tramways in the Gloucester, Cheltenham and Stroud area. This led to a GWR report being made in December 1902 which recommended introducing an efficient local rail service between Chalford and Stonehouse as an alternative to the proposed tramway.

As early as October 1901, the GWR's general manager, Sir

Joseph Wilkinson, was anxious that the company should be first in the railcar field. The locomotive engineer, William Dean, began work but was soon superseded by Churchward, who probably considered the project less important than his planned developments with larger locomotives.

The LSWR/LB&SCR railcar No. 2 was borrowed over a weekend but, being designed for a 1¼-mile-long branch, was unsuited to the 7-mile-long and hilly Gloucestershire run, and with a load of thirty passengers its speed did not exceed 8 mph on the gradient or 27 mph on the level. Churchward promised that a GWR rail motor would overcome these problems.

The first GWR car entered service on 12 October 1903 and accommodated fifty-two passengers. They entered through a vestibule provided with steps so passengers could enter or alight at level crossings. It proved a success, and on the first Saturday of working about 5,000 passengers were carried, two cars running coupled together. A unique feature of the GWR scheme was stopping at level crossings, the object being to enable the company to pick up and drop passengers close to their homes in a similar way to an electric tram car.

The level crossing stopping places proved popular and became 'halts', economically built, unstaffed platforms with simple shelters. The GWR also introduced another category of station: a 'platform', similar to a halt but staffed for at least part of the day.

The rail motors proved successful up to a point, but were limited in capacity and therefore required the substitution of a normal train on market days or fair days, or when a major sporting event was taking place. The answer was an auto (or push-and-pull) train consisting of coaches with a driving end and an ordinary steam locomotive. The engine pulled the coaches in the normal manner on the outward journey, but when the terminus was reached the engine stayed at the same end, which then became the rear, and then pushed the train, the driver controlling the engine from a control compartment at what had now become the front of the train. The fireman remained on the footplate. Auto trains lasted on the Western and Southern Regions of British Railways until the 1960s.

In the nineteenth century, most railwaymen worked a basic twelve-hour day and, as long as rules were not infringed, held a job for life. However, various factors could lengthen the day – for instance, fog or snow might delay trains – and in most cases no overtime was paid. Double-shift working was required by one set of signalmen at a weekly or fortnightly changeover of shifts. The excessive time worked by signalmen and drivers led to accidents caused by tiredness.

In 1871, Michael Bass, MP and brewer, raised the matter in Parliament and revealed that some Midland drivers had, during the previous two months, worked an average of nineteen and a half hours instead of ten. In 1893, the Railway Servants' Hours of Labour Act provided for the Board of Trade to inquire into complaints of overwork.

Being a railwayman was dangerous: in 1906, 27 out of every 10,000 goods guards and shunters employed lost their lives in the course of their work, while 26 out of every 10,000 shunters were killed while on duty, the work of these grades being twice as dangerous as being a miner.

Many railway companies were very considerate to their employees, the Great Western perhaps being the most outstanding. It provided far more than just housing facilities. George Gibbs, a director, left money in his will towards building a church and school for Swindon. The Mechanics' Institute was built to provide facilities for mutual improvement classes, a library (no municipal library was provided in Swindon until 1943) and a theatre. The

GWR medical fund provided doctors' surgeries and a dispensary, and by 1948 the GWR Medical Fund Hospital could deal with a population of 40,000. The GWR had its own hearse and supplied coal and timber to its employees at advantageous prices. The GWR provided a park, and both Turkish and swimming baths.

One of the features of Swindon works was the annual trip. It started in 1849, when 500 workmen travelled to Oxford by special train, and by 1908 on trip day no less than 24,564 left Swindon in twenty-two special trains for various destinations. If it was wet, they sheltered in the trains all day. In 1913, employees could go away for a whole week instead of just a day. In 1939, 27,000 left Swindon in thirty trains. Trip week was really a lockout for workmen until a week's paid holiday was given in 1938.

# 10

# Principal Pre-Grouping Railways

The Barry Railway was one of the last independent railway companies created in the nineteenth century. It opened for traffic at the end of 1888 with about ten engines and by the end of the century the locomotive stud numbered 126.

The company came into being because colliery owners in the Aberdare and Rhondda valleys who exported coal through Cardiff and Penarth found that dock accommodation was insufficient and coal was sometimes kept for weeks in the colliery companies' wagons before it could be loaded into ships.

Some of the larger colliery owners decided to raise capital for a new port at Barry. Although owning less than 70 route miles, the Barry Railway was a highly important and prosperous system and in the record year of 1913 carried over 11 million tons of coal and coke.

Its most interesting engines were the D class 0-8-0s, which were, apart from a primitive engine of this wheel arrangement built for the Monmouthshire Railway & Canal Company in 1847, the first British eight-coupled engine.

Built by Sharp, Stewart & Co. for the Swedish & Norwegian Railway, but when that line proved so expensive to construct that the company ran out of funds two 0-8-0s intended for the line remained in the maker's hands and were sold to the Barry Railway in 1889. Sixteen engines from Sweden were returned to the makers in the early 1890s, some then being resold elsewhere, leaving two in the hands of Sharp, Stewart & Co. These were offered to the Barry Railway and delivered in 1897. The Barry Railway had a more liberal loading gauge than some railways, so the outside cylinders had to be removed for the journey from the maker's works. The tenders of all the 0-8-0s were of the four-wheel type, to which the Barry Railway added well tanks to increase the rather limited water capacity.

For heavy mineral traffic, seven particularly heavy 0-8-2Ts were built in 1897 by Sharp, Stewart & Co., this representing another new wheel arrangement for Britain. They competently handled loads of eighty to a hundred wagons.

The railway badly needed more engines in 1899, and, as British builders were unable to accept orders due to a strike, ten 0-6-2Ts were obtained from abroad: five from the Franco-Belge Co. of Belgium and five from the Cooke Locomotive Co., New Jersey. The latter five were a combination of British and American practice. Tests showed that the coal and water consumption was greater than the British engines. They were said to have required two or three water stops when taking empties up the Rhondda Valley and, as one old driver put it, 'you dare not pass a single water column with the Yankees'. All were withdrawn by May 1932, but the Belgian-built engines lasted into the British Railways era, the last being withdrawn in 1951.

The Caledonian Railway was originally anticipated to be the only railway between England and Scotland, so branches at Carstairs served both Glasgow and Edinburgh. By amalgamation with other companies, it reached Aberdeen and Oban. The

Caledonian ran fast trains connecting with its fast steamer services. Its locomotives, rolling stock and stations were some of the best in the country. The Lanarkshire coalfield, one of the richest in Scotland, was almost exclusively served by the Caledonian, as were the Clyde shipyards and steelworks.

The Cambrian Railways, unusual for being in the plural, was the largest of the Welsh companies in terms of route mileage and area covered before being absorbed into the Great Western. It was formed on 25 July 1864 from a union of four railways and had a main line 95¾ miles long from Whitchurch to Aberystwyth and reached Pwllheli in 1867. The Cambrian Railways largely covered central Wales and included two narrow gauge systems: the 1 foot 11½ inch gauge Vale of Rheidol and the 2 foot 6 inch Welshpool and Llanfair. The Cambrian totalled 300 miles of rural railway. The company's headquarters was at Oswestry. The railway tended to suffer from poor timekeeping, partly due to the single track with passing loops and partly because railways feeding it handed over late trains, the London & North Western being a particular culprit.

The Glasgow & South Western Railway, as its name implied, served the country south-west of Glasgow and provided an alternative route between Glasgow and Carlisle via Dumfries. This had the advantage that it was 300 feet lower than the Caledonian's route, but the disadvantage that it was 18 miles longer. When the Midland Railway opened its Settle & Carlisle line in 1876, Midland trains to Scotland used the Glasgow & South Western route. As the Midland could not compete with the East and West Coast routes on distance, it promoted the route on its superior standards of comfort. The Glasgow & South Western also owned part of the Anglo-Irish route from Carlisle, through Dumfries to Stranraer.

Patrick Stirling, its chief locomotive engineer, preferred to see a single-wheeler rather than a coupled engine at the head of his expresses, once remarking that a coupled engine at high speed reminded him of 'a laddie runnin' wi' his breeks down'. When asked by William Stroudley why he did not use domed boilers, his reply was to the effect that he would not tolerate anything resembling a chamber pot on his engines.

The Great Central was the newest of the principal railway companies. Origination was from the Manchester, Sheffield & Lincolnshire Railway, which had Edward Watkin as its chairman, a very go-ahead character who also became chairman of other lines, including the South Eastern and the Metropolitan Railways. A visionary, Watkin was an early advocate of the Channel Tunnel.

To fulfil this dream, the Manchester, Sheffield & Lincolnshire was to be extended to London and then reach the tunnel over other lines of which he was chairman. He had the foresight to build the extension to the Continental loading gauge. The Great Central, as it had then been renamed, reached its terminus in London, Marylebone, in 1899. As it served towns which already had a direct route to London, it diluted traffic from other lines.

Its locomotive and carriage works were established at Gorton; a new port was built at Immingham and a hump marshalling yard at Wath to deal with South Yorkshire coal. The Great Central set up through passenger coach workings to destinations on other railways, sometimes Great Central engines working throughout. Early in the twentieth century it worked a train from Manchester to Plymouth via Oxford a trip of 374 miles each way. Jointly with the Great Western, in 1906 it constructed a second route to London via Princes Risborough and High Wycombe.

Primarily a goods line, less than a quarter of its receipts came from passengers. As much of its main line duplicated others, many miles were closed in the 1960s, proving the adage that the last to be built was the first to go.

British locomotive builders were unable to accept new orders in 1899 due to an engineering strike, so the Great Central commissioned twenty 2-6-0s to be built by the Baldwin Works in the USA. Costing £2,600 each, they came over in parts which were assembled at the Great Central's Gorton works. The locomotives' appearance was an amalgam of British and American design but they had US-style bogie tenders. Officially designated Class 15, locomotive crews referred to them as 'Yankees'. One was completely wrecked in a collision between a coal train and a fish train at Brocklesby, Lincolnshire, on 28 March 1907. Most of the others were withdrawn before the First World War, and the final member of the class scrapped before June 1915.

Due to the coal strike between April and June 1921, a few new engines built at Gorton were temporarily equipped to burn oil using Holden's system, a few others being fitted with the Great Central's chief locomotive engineer J. G. Robinson's own system, Unoleo.

This was not the company's first effort with alternative fuel, as in July 1917 a 2-8-0 was adapted to burn pulverised fuel, its standard tender being fitted with the necessary container and gear. In January 1920, another 2-8-0 was adapted for burning a mixture of 60 per cent pulverised coal and 40 per cent oil described as colloidal fuel. The experiments continued after Grouping but ended in February 1924 as the cost of pulverising the coal outweighed any economy derived from using a lower grade of fuel.

A serious danger in a railway accident is that one coach may ride up on another and smash it. Robinson designed interlocking fenders to prevent this. Above each coach buffer was a corrugated block which in the event of a derailment would lock into a facing one and prevent a coach rising.

The Great Eastern Railway had a monopoly east of Cambridge and operated dense working-class suburban traffic at Liverpool Street and, moreover, kept to time. It conveyed vast quantities of fish from Lowestoft and Yarmouth, served the Low Countries from Harwich and had many significant holiday resorts in its territory. It also served Newmarket. In 1872, it offered third-class accommodation on all trains and in 1891 was the first British company to allow third-class passengers to use a restaurant car. When traffic increased to more than Harwich could handle, Parkeston Quay was opened in 1883, named after the company's chairman, C. H. Parkes.

In 1920 it reorganised its suburban system, and, to aid passengers in finding the right class of compartment, first- and second-class coaches bore yellow and blue stripes, hence the nickname 'jazz trains'.

The Great North of Scotland Railway covered the County of Aberdeen. At Aberdeen itself the Caledonian and Great North of Scotland stations were nearly a mile apart, and the Great North timed the departure of its trains from Aberdeen so close to the arrival of trains from Perth and the south that passengers for Inverness had hardly any chance of catching them unless they had no luggage and could sprint. The officials seemed to wait until the hurrying passengers were in sight, then slammed the gates and started the train.

Much of the Great North's traffic was local, but it stimulated tourism by opening a hotel at Cruden Bay in 1899, served by an electric tramway from the local railway station. Special fish trains were run and concessionary fares offered to stimulate fish sellers travelling inland.

The Great North never operated second-class carriages and so beat the Midland to this by almost twenty years. It labelled carriages 'third' and then cannily charged fares, which lay somewhere between first and second in amount.

James Manson, its chief locomotive engineer, invented an automatic tablet exchanger for single-line working. It was essential after the introduction of fast trains, which stopped only at principal stations, as an apparatus was required to carry out tablet exchange at a speed higher than could be achieved by hand.

A cast-iron post stood at the side of the line, just far enough back to clear the engine and train. On this were mounted two forks for delivering and receiving the tablets to and from the engine. The receiving fork had strong prongs which faced the approaching train, while the delivery fork had weaker prongs facing in the opposite direction, towards which the train was travelling.

On the engine was a similar exchanger, with picking-up and delivery forks attached to an arm. The engine and station forks were at a slightly different level in order not to foul each other.

As the engine passed, the strong receiving fork on the station platform caught the leather pouch containing the tablet which the engine carried in the reversed weak fork, while at the same time the strong fork on the engine picked up a new tablet pouch lightly held by the reversed weak fork on the platform. It is greatly to Manson's credit that he refused to patent his invention, leaving it to be applied freely by any railway in the hope that it would help protect railway servants from the injury liable to occur with the old method of exchange by hand.

The Great Northern's main line ran from King's Cross to York and the company's main works was established at Doncaster. It had access to all the important West Yorkshire towns. In 1860, the East Coast Joint Stock was established with other companies, a common pool of passenger vehicles for working Anglo-Scottish trains. The 10.00 a.m. departures from King's Cross and Edinburgh began in 1862 and by ten years later were known as the Flying Scotsman. The company's main income was from freight, especially coal traffic, and it was the pioneer of fully braked goods trains.

Some of the East Coast stock in the early 1900s was articulated. This was a system by which the ends of coaches shared a bogie. This had the advantages of being cheaper and giving less weight for a locomotive to pull, but had the disadvantage that a fault, for instance a hot box on one coach, could put the rest of the set out of use.

The Great Western Railway, originally just a line from London to Bristol, reached Penzance and eventually served much of England south of a line from Birkenhead to London. In Wales it mostly just ran along the south coast and then up the west coast as far as Aberystwyth.

The Great Western was known for its broad gauge of 7 feet ¼ inch. In theory this was fine, but when railway systems developed it prevented through running. The difficulty was partly solved by adding a third rail at the standard gauge distance, thus making a mixed gauge track.

At the beginning of the twentieth century, its locomotive engineer, George Churchward, produced splendid standardised engines which lasted until the end of the company. The GWR was the pioneer of a warning system whereby a driver received an audible warning of an adverse signal, invaluable in fog.

The Highland Railway ran to the Kyle of Lochalsh, Wick and Thurso. Due to the sparsity of traffic, in 1914 it only possessed

47 miles of double track, much of this being passing loops. Mixed trains were a common sight, at one time even running a Pullman sleeper on a mixed train. The company was plagued by snow in winter and sparks catching lineside vegetation alight in summer. The line enjoyed heavy traffic around 12 August for the opening of the grouse-shooting season, while during the First World War the line was invaluable for carrying coal for the fleet at Scapa Flow.

Although a small company in terms of route miles, the Lancashire & Yorkshire Railway, or the 'Lanky' as it was familiarly known, worked dense traffic and the number of locomotives it owned placed it fourth nationally in the size of its locomotive stud. Apart from its Manchester to Liverpool route, which competed with the London & North Western, it enjoyed a monopoly of traffic in many districts. It owned Fleetwood docks jointly with the London & North Western, while from Goole it ran shipping services to the Continent. In 1903 the company introduced the country's first electro-pneumatic signalling, while an interesting provision for Manchester businessmen wishing to enjoy sea, rather than industrial air, was the Blackpool and Southport 'club' trains.

These were introduced in 1895, when first-class season ticket holders approached the company and asked that an exclusive coach be provided morning and evening when a certain number of annual seasons were purchased. A supplementary fee was charged to club members and they enjoyed their own seats, usually armchairs. One rule was that all windows were to be kept closed while the train was moving.

It was one of the first railways in Britain to introduce electrification to suburban lines. Multiple unit operation started in March 1904 on the Liverpool and Southport line, while two years later the Liverpool to Aintree line was electrified.

The London & North Western Railway, calling itself 'the Premier Line', was formed by the amalgamation of the Grand Junction, London & Birmingham and Manchester & Birmingham Railways. It joined other lines linked to Carlisle and so was part of the West Coast route to Scotland. By 1859, the LNWR had extended to Cambridge, Holyhead, Leeds, Oxford and Peterborough. Eight years later it owned most of the route through central Wales between Shrewsbury and Swansea. From Hereford it had running powers to Newport and Cardiff.

It was a company which had competition – the East Coast route competed for Scottish traffic, while the GWR also enjoyed routes to Birmingham, Shrewsbury and Birkenhead, the latter being convenient for Liverpool. The Lancashire & Yorkshire owned a rival line between Manchester and Liverpool. One of the three largest railways in Britain, it called itself 'the largest joint-stock company in the world' and prided itself on having 'the finest permanent way in the world'. In the early 1900s, its publicity department produced over 11 million postcards depicting the company's locomotives, trains and stations. Its dividend was rarely below 6 per cent.

LNWR locomotives were built at Crewe, coaches at Wolverton and wagons at Earlestown, near Warrington. One of its locomotive engineers, Francis Webb, pioneered compound locomotives in Britain and made extensive use of 0-8-0s for freight haulage. The company was up to date and as early as 1882 used gravity to shunt at Liverpool. In order to separate fast and slow trains, most of the 209 miles between Euston and Preston were either quadrupled, or had double-track alternative routes. Pre-1914, the company introduced club trains morning and evening between Llandudno and other North Wales resorts and Liverpool and Manchester.

The London & South Western Railway had its London terminus at the rather remote location of Nine Elms and in 1848 built an expensive 1¾-mile-long extension to Waterloo. In addition to its suburban lines, the LSWR covered much of the territory between Salisbury, Portsmouth and Exeter, while beyond was the 'Withered Arm', serving North Devon and North Cornwall.

From Southampton, a port it developed, the LSWR ran steamers to the Channel Islands and France, while from Lymington it operated a ferry to Yarmouth on the Isle of Wight. Jointly with the Midland Railway it owned the Somerset & Dorset Railway, thus giving it valuable links to and from the North.

The London & South Western, not serving any collieries or iron fields, was primarily a passenger-carrying line and offered consistent dividends. Between 1902 and 1907, the earliest British automatic pneumatic signals controlled by track circuits were installed between Woking and Basingstoke.

The London, Brighton & South Coast Railway operated in the triangle between London, Portsmouth and Eastbourne, with cross-channel services from Newhaven. Its principal passenger trains were between London and Brighton, Pullman cars running on some of these services from 1875, with the very first electrically lit railway coach in the world, named *Globe*, from 1881. These trains enabled Sussex to become a London dormitory. The first slip coach in Britain dropped off the rear of a passenger train at Haywards Heath in 1858. As LB&SCR lines were relatively short, the company made great use of tank engines. It is believed that the LB&SCR was the first to adopt flying junctions, whereby one line crossed another by a bridge, rather than using a flat junction which could delay other trains.

Brighton expresses did not always live up to their name. In

the late nineteenth century a London & North Western fish train ran the 53 miles from Tebay to Preston at a speed of 47.4 mph; a Brighton express ran the 50½ miles from London to Brighton at 46.6 mph. It was better to be a dead mackerel on the North Western than a first-class passenger on the Brighton line!

The Metropolitan Railway was a fascinating line due to its wide variety. It was the world's first passenger-carrying underground railway and opened between Paddington and Farringdon Street on 10 January 1863. It was constructed by the simple but chaos-causing method of digging a deep, wide trench in a street, laying track and then putting a roof on, a system known as cut-and-cover.

Originally broad gauge as it was allied to the Great Western, it became standard gauge in 1867. By 1884, it had been extended to form, with the Metropolitan District Railway, a circle linking the principal main-line termini north of the Thames by offering the Great Northern, London, Chatham & Dover and the Midland trains access to the city. Despite such measures as condensing used steam to make conditions underground that much pleasanter, electrification in 1905 was the answer.

What was truly amazing was that the Metropolitan Railway ran trains to Wotton in the depths of rural Buckinghamshire. The single-track branch from Quainton Road to Wotton was opened 1 April 1871 using horse traction and extended to Brill the following year. Relaid with heavier track for locomotive working, the Metropolitan Railway took over operation on 1 December 1899. The London Passenger Transport Board, formed in 1933, made the decision not to run trains beyond Aylesbury, so the branch closed from 1 December 1935.

The Brill branch was not the furthest extent of the Metropolitan Railway – this was Verney Junction on the Oxford to Cambridge line. The station built by the Aylesbury & Verney

Junction Railway opened 23 September 1868. The Aylesbury & Buckingham directors, anxious to sell to a larger concern, made overtures to the Great Western, but that company was tardy and Sir Edward Watkins, chairman of the Metropolitan Railway, anxious for his company to expand north, took it over in 1890 as part of a projected link from the Manchester, Sheffield & Lincolnshire Railway, via the Metropolitan to the South Eastern Railway and a Channel Tunnel. The Metropolitan improved the Verney Junction line and doubled it. Eventually it became part of the Great Central's London extension. Waddesdon Manor station was used by Lord Rothschild, owner of the manor, the Metropolitan Railway building him a special saloon from two old compartment coaches. Verney Junction was frequently used by Florence Nightingale when making visits to Sir Harry Verney at Claydon House. In 1922, eight trains ran over the line daily, including one Pullman service, either with a car named *Mayflower* or with *Galatea*. Six of the trains ran through to Baker Street or Liverpool Street. Baker Street was 50½ miles from Verney Junction. In 1936, Metropolitan trains stopped running north of Aylesbury.

The Metropolitan operated like a main-line railway and provided three passenger classes, reduced to two in 1905; it also handled freight and parcels traffic. It sought traffic by developing housing along its line using the slogan 'Metro-land'.

The Midland Railway, centred on Derby, was an amalgamation of the Birmingham & Derby Junction, the Midland Counties and the North Midland Railways, and was the first large amalgamation sanctioned by Parliament. It was an expansionist company and projected lines to Lincoln, Morecambe and Peterborough; then it grabbed the Birmingham–Gloucester–Bristol line, thus gaining the heart of Great Western territory. It laid a branch to Bath and then, jointly with the London & South Western, seized the Somerset & Dorset Railway from under the nose of the Great Western and thus reached Bournemouth.

The Midland first accessed London by means of running powers over the Great Northern to King's Cross. This proved unsatisfactory, so it built its own line with a splendid terminus designed by Gilbert Scott at St Pancras and which opened in 1868. The massive single-arch train shed was exceeded only by three others, built later in the USA. Trains use the first floor, the cellar originally used to store beer and the pillars supporting the floor above being spaced to allow the maximum number of barrels to be stored.

The Midland, casting envious eyes at the profits earned by the East and West Coast routes, decided to have its own railway and so built the Settle & Carlisle line, which filled the missing link between its existing line and Carlisle. From there it used the Glasgow & South Western to reach Glasgow and Edinburgh, hence the phrase 'St George for England; St Pancras for Scotland'.

To attract passengers to its routes, which were not always as the crow flies, in 1872 the Midland lured passengers by carrying third-class passengers in all trains, while three years later it discontinued second class, reducing first-class fares and improving third-class accommodation to the former second-class standard. In 1874, the Midland operated the first Pullman cars in Britain, a supplementary fare being paid to enjoy this luxury. Warmed by an oil-fired heater, it also had water closets and lavatories served by force pumps from low-level tanks. Not without reason, the company called itself 'The Best Way'. The Pullman cars were of an American design, saloon and not compartment, with straight rather than curved sides with large, square-cornered windows. Their vestibules had inward-opening doors.

Derby works was rarely capable of supplying the company's full needs for new engines and quite a few were built by outside British suppliers. In 1899, British builders had full order books so the Midland was forced to seek elsewhere and initially ordered twenty engines from Baldwin Works in the United States 'equal to the Standard Class 2 goods engine'. The order was then doubled, but Baldwin Works was also busy and could only provide a total of thirty, the remaining ten being built by Schenectady. The Schenectady tenders had a new lease of life when in 1917 they were coupled to new Class 4 4-4-0s.

The American engines were 2-6-0s rather than 0-6-0s and all were delivered in 1899. The Baldwins were of typical American appearance and had bogie tenders, but those built by Schenectady had a more British appearance and six-wheel tenders. They enjoyed but a short life; all the Baldwins were withdrawn by 1914 and the Schenectady by August 1915. They were unpopular with crews despite their cabs giving more weather protection than English engines, but perhaps there was a feeling that an American engine should be much bigger and more powerful than a British one, which they were not, and by Derby standards they were roughly built. S. W. Johnson, the Midland's locomotive engineer, wrote that they consumed twenty to 25 per cent more coal and 50 per cent more oil than his standard 0-6-0s, while repairs cost 60 per cent more. He did, however, say that 'there is another point. The Americans were delivered here within a few months of the order being given, yet some contracts which we let out to British firms in 1897 were not completed until February 1900! Of course, that was largely the fault of the engineering strike, and it was the engineering strike which caused us to put out work in America.'

The Midland was a 'small engine' line, preferring to run short and frequent services rather than longer ones less frequently and adopting double-heading of its heavier trains rather than constructing larger engines. This policy resulted in the company running some of the last single-driving-wheel engines in the country, and, unlike other large companies, it never owned a six-coupled express engine. In addition to passenger trains, the Midland carried much heavy freight traffic, particularly coal, to London.

The Midland & South Western Junction Railway linked the Midland Railway at Cheltenham with the London & South Western at Andover, though its first few miles at the northern end were from running powers over the Great Western's Cheltenham to Banbury line. The company had two noteworthy locomotive types. The first was a 0-4-4T with a Fairlie double bogie. Although at first glance an ordinary 0-4-4T, the driving wheels were in fact on a bogie. Built in 1878, it was shown that year at the Paris Exhibition. In 1882 it was sold to the Swindon, Marlborough & Andover Railway (one of the forerunners of the MSWJR) for £1,000. It was one of the first engines in Britain to be fitted with Walschaerts valve gear and proved very heavy on coal, thus was only used when the line was very short of engine power.

The other noteworthy engines were two 2-6-0s built for a South American railway, and these were among the first engines of this wheel arrangement to run in Britain.

The North British Railway was promoted to build a line from Edinburgh to Dunbar and Berwick and thus form part of the East Coast route. Another line formed the Waverley route from Edinburgh to Carlisle. The company was in financial doldrums until matters improved when the Midland opened the Settle & Carlisle route as the North British worked trains from Carlisle to Edinburgh. The company's great rival was the Caledonian, and they competed not just with rail services but also with steamer services. Waverley station at Edinburgh was highly congested until remodelled and extended in 1898, when it was said to have more platform accommodation than any other station in Britain except for Waterloo.

The North British operated a horse-worked branch until 1914, when it changed to locomotive working. This was the 2½-mile-long Port Carlisle line, situated on the English side of the border, so the company probably considered horse traction quite good enough for southerners.

In 1915 a new naval dockyard opened at Rosyth and in 1918 the North British carried over 1¼ million tons of Welsh coal there, in addition to special trains for ships' crews.

The North Eastern Railway, with its headquarters at York, formed part of the East Coast route. The company was sluggish in introducing safety systems such as the block and the interlocking of points and signals; in fact, when the board discovered that its manager, William O'Brien, had neglected this aspect of his responsibility, he was sacked.

The North Eastern was individualist; long after other companies were using steel rail, the company still utilised iron. Then, when the Railway Clearing House was discussing a revision of telegraphic codes in 1883, its passenger superintendent, Alexander Christison, stated, 'As I could not possibly agree to any alteration of our code, I think it is unnecessary to have anyone at the meeting to represent the North Eastern company.'

The company depended largely on heavy mineral traffic and so was susceptible to variations in trade. The North Eastern was the first railway to negotiate directly with a trade union on wages and hours of work; contemporary companies tried to ignore the unions. Another innovation was electrifying the Newcastle Quayside line in 1902 and the Tyne suburban system two years later – well before the electrification of surface lines in London. Plans were being formulated for electrifying the main line between York and Newcastle for all traffic, but then the First World War prevented them from being carried out and they were not implemented until 1991.

The Rhymney Railway, originally 51 miles of single track from Cardiff to Merthyr, Dowlais and Rhymney, was doubled in the 1870s to cope with the increasing traffic and the company paid excellent dividends. Cutting the 1,193-yard-long Caerphilly Tunnel took five years. Sand and water pouring in proved a problem, so consequently the tunnel was lined throughout. The water was piped to Cardiff for locomotive use.

Regulations for working Down trains through Caerphilly Tunnel were very stringent. No goods or mineral train was allowed to enter the tunnel from its north end at a speed greater than 6 mph; sufficient brakes had to be pinned down to compel driver to use a little steam in passing through the tunnel, but the speed on emerging from the south end was not to exceed 4 mph.

Braking coal trains descending the valleys needed considerable skill. Sufficient wagon brakes had to be pinned down to keep the train under control, but it was strictly forbidden to allow a wheel to skid and disobedience meant that the guard and brakesman would be severely punished. To prevent brake blocks from burning, when descending a bank drivers had to keep their rail water taps open and guards were instructed to put the fire out if any brake blocks were found to be burning at the bottom of the incline.

In 1889, the Rhymney suffered some loss of traffic when the opening of the Barry Railway took some of its traffic. In 1909 and 1910, the Taff Vale Railway tried to absorb the Rhymney Railway and the Cardiff Railway, but Parliament would not assent to this move. However, both the Rhymney and the Cardiff railways surmounted this problem by having the Taff Vale's manager supervising their companies.

One of the unusual characteristics of the Rhymney company was Cornelius Lundie, its general manager for over forty years, who seemingly controlled the railway single handed. Not only was he general manger, he was also traffic manager, superintendent of the line, chief engineer and chief locomotive superintendent. He retired, probably contrary to his wishes, shortly before his ninetieth birthday and was appointed consulting director until his death three years later. He claimed to be the oldest railway director in the world and was also believed to have been the last surviving person to have known Sir Walter Scott personally.

The fact of him holding several posts could produce problems. If private wagons were found with defective brakes, a guard, whose duty it was to examine them before they left the sidings, had to report the matter to the manager's office immediately on arrival at Cardiff. The manager was superintendent of the line and would not have been pleased had an important wagon been left behind. On the other hand, had the wheels on a faulty wagon skidded that guard would have received 'severe punishment' from the same Lundie wearing a different hat!

The South Eastern & Chatham Railway was formed in 1899 by a union of the South Eastern Railway and the London, Chatham & Dover Railway. The South Eastern Railway was the first principal railway in Kent. Initially it worked into London over the metals of three other railways. It reached Folkestone in 1843 and Dover the following year and gradually covered all of Kent. It operated ships to the Continent, and until 1880 the times of the boat train varied daily according to the tide. This led to the Staplehurst accident, where Charles Dickens was injured. Sir

Edward Watkin became chairman of the company in 1866 and sought to build a Channel tunnel.

The South Eastern was none too popular with its passengers, and this led to E. L. Ahrons, in *Locomotive and Train Working in the Latter Part of the Nineteenth Century* (1917), writing,

> The South Eastern of twenty-five to thirty years ago was a railway combining a number of good features with many exceedingly bad ones, and at one time, in company with its younger Chatham brother and rival, was held in the estimation of the local travelling public to be —. Here the reader had better choose his own adjectives, of which a choice and lurid selection was at one time to be obtained from most regular passengers on the line, except those connected with churches.

The London, Chatham & Dover Railway entered into severe competition with the South Eastern Railway. It came into being due to the South Eastern reaching Dover via the Weald instead of extending its Medway line. Although the Chatham company had no major accidents between 1878 and 1898, it was not endeared to some of its passengers, who referred to it as the 'London, Smash'em & Turn Over Railway'.

The South Eastern & Chatham ran Pullman stock in some its Channel ferry trains and opened a new dockside station, Dover Marine, in 1919. Some of its suburban coaches were not above criticism.

The Taff Vale Railway was the largest, oldest and most prosperous of the six constituent companies joining the GWR in 1922 – it paid its shareholders 17.5 per cent one year. The Taff Vale was authorised in 1836 to construct a 24-mile-long line between Merthyr and Cardiff. It was engineered by Brunel, who preferred standard gauge for the curving lines along the Taff Vale. It opened in 1841 and also served the Rhondda Valley. Although the company had over 100 route miles, no express trains were run. As miners' clothes were none too clean, like all railways carrying this class of traffic, the Taff Vale supplied stock without cushions.

A particularly interesting feature was its Pwllyrhebog branch, with its incline of 1 in 13. This demanded a special locomotive and cables. The incline, about 1¾ miles in length, began with half a mile of 1 in 13, the remainder being at 1 in 29/30.

Empty wagons were raised up the incline by a cable which passed round a drum at the top and was connected to a descending loaded train. To avoid troublesome breakaways, a locomotive propelled wagons up the incline, the cable passing below the wagons to connect with the engine.

Old locomotives were utilised until 1844, but that year the locomotive superintendent, Tom Riches, designed special 0-6-0T engines. Their wheels were standard with passenger classes in order to allow the axles sufficient clearance for the cable and haulage gear. In addition to steam brakes on all the wheels, a slipper brake was provided between the driving and trailing wheels. The engines normally worked up the incline bunker first, a steeply sloping firebox crown ensuring an even depth of water above, yet if a locomotive had to proceed chimney first then the design allowed the crown to remain fully covered.

A few other engines were subsequently fitted with haulage equipment, such as a 0-6-2T and a 0-6-0PT. The incline closed in 1951 and all three original engines were withdrawn within two years. Despite the short length of the branch, the engine with the highest mileage achieved 943,197 miles in its sixty-eight years of use.

At some time before 1913, two tenders were employed to act as a counterbalance for ascending trains when a loaded train was unavailable at the top, later being joined by a third. They probably ceased work in 1932.

On any railway, very few accidents were caused by locomotive faults. In August 1893, a link holding the spring on one of the driving wheels of 4-4-2T No. 173 fractured, with the result that the spring became detached and was dragged along beneath the engine until it got under the wheels of the leading van of the train, derailing it and the rest of the train. Thirteen people died.

Until the end of 1885, when the first of the company's 0-6-2Ts appeared, nearly all of its mineral trains were worked by tender engines. Although for about half of their lives the tender engines worked tender first, over steeply graded lines they had the great advantage that almost double the brake power was available, because in addition to the engine's brakes there were those of the tender.

E. L. Ahrons, in *Locomotive and Train Working in the Latter Part of the Nineteenth Century*, wrote that between 1887 and 1890 he observed a large number of Taff Vale coal trains entering Cardiff without rear brake vans. Frequently a number of wagon brakes were pinned down, but in all such cases tender and not tank engines were employed. Whenever a tank engine was used, there was always a brake van at the rear of the train.

The first national railway strike took place on 15 August 1911, when the railway unions gave the companies twenty-four hours to decide whether they would meet union representatives to negotiate a settlement as railwaymen felt that their pay had fallen behind that of other workers. The companies, backed by the government, which offered to supply troops to help run the railways, declared they would rather face a strike than negotiate a settlement. Some

200,000 railwaymen ceased work, threatening the jobs of other workers dependent on coal. Two rioters were shot dead by the Army at Llanelli, and this action caused public opinion to side with the strikers. A Royal Commission of Inquiry was set up within two days, and the strike was called off. The report appeared in October, and modest wage increases were made in December to most railwaymen, some having their hours of work decreased.

In the Edwardian Age, most towns and villages were within about 2 miles of a station, this being a convenient distance for collection and delivery by horse. Practically every station had its goods yard as the railway was by law a 'common carrier', meaning that it was required to carry anything offered to it. This proved a serious disadvantage when road transport developed because lorry owners could cherry-pick the most profitable traffic, leaving the least profitable to be carried by the railways. By 1900, Britain had about 21,500 route miles of railway.

N. L. R.
Available day of issue only
O.W to
1 3 O.W to FORD
1d Third Class 1d
Issued subject to the Company's
Published Regulations.
K
Old Ford          Old Ford
13 MR 98          9630

N. L. R.
Available for 7 Days
INTERCHANGE
Privilege Ticket
OUTWARD HALF
THIRD CLASS
ACTON
To
on          By
via
I.P.T) Fare          2152

N. L. R. Return
Available day of issue or
from Saturday to Monday
BROAD STREET
to HIGHBURY
& ISLINGTON (S.9
6
3d 3rd. Class
Not transferable
Issued subject to the
Company's Published
Regulations.
914

# 11

# The First World War and Its Aftermath

Railways have always proved useful to governments in time of war. As early as 1834, when the London & Southampton Railway was seeking its Bill in Parliament, the promoters used a general, an admiral and five Royal Navy captains to support their proposal. In the event of civil disobedience, troops could be sent rapidly by rail to any part of the country; quite a contrast to 1806, when the government chartered canal boats to carry troops from London to Liverpool in seven days instead of the fourteen required had they marched.

The invasion scare of 1859 suggested armoured trains for coastal defence and in 1871 the government obtained powers for taking over railways in wartime.

During the South African War of 1899–1902, railways, mostly the London & South Western, handled military traffic in liaison with the War Office and the Admiralty. Some 528,000 troops with their horses and equipment left from Southampton.

When the War Office decided to establish a permanent military site on Salisbury Plain, the LSWR applied for a Light Railway Order to construct the Amesbury & Military Camp Light Railway. Unlike most light railways, which followed the lie of the land, it had embankments up to 35 feet high and cuttings 38 feet deep. It opened to military traffic in 1901 and to public passengers on 2 June 1902, the first train bringing the morning papers with the joyful news that the South African War was over. The line was later extended to two more camps. Further camps were set up on the outbreak of the First World War, along with several more railway extensions, including Flying Shed sidings and to Fargo Hospital.

A new military camp was also set up at Tidworth on the Hampshire/Wiltshire border and was linked to the Midland & South Western Junction Railway at Ludgershall. Opened in 1901, the station at Tidworth was literally on the county boundary – when buying a ticket, the passenger stood in Hampshire while the booking clerk was in Wiltshire. Receipts at Tidworth, the only MSWJR station lit by electricity, were the highest on the system, and the station was in the charge of the highest-ranking station master. The camp had its own railway system worked by a variety of locomotives. The seven sidings in the yard held 290 wagons, or ten trains of twelve coaches.

Longmoor Camp was initiated in 1900 to provide accommodation for soldiers returning from the South African War. The first railway troops, the 53rd Railway Company of the Royal Engineers, arrived in May 1903 to transport huts from Longmoor to Bordon, a distance of five miles. They were moved by the ingenious method of using two parallel narrow gauge tracks about 24 feet apart to carry trolleys, on which the huts were carried. Haulage was by cable and steam winch.

In 1905, a parallel standard gauge line was laid to connect with the Bordon Light Railway. Standard gauge traffic began on the Woolmer Instructional Military Railway in 1908, and in 1933 its name changed to the Longmoor Military Railway. Apart from carrying supplies to the camp, the line had the purpose of training railwaymen for military working. As well as for regular soldiers, it was used for the annual summer camp training of the Supplementary Reserve Units recruited from the railway companies.

The First World War had a great effect on railways. Many special naval and military trains were run, including ambulance trains. The railways were required to carry arms and munitions, all this work extra to normal transport and carried out with less men because many had joined the forces. For the first time women became an important part of a railway – from just over 13,000 before the war, the total rose to 34,000 eighteen months later, and 52,000 by September 1918.

British companies had to supply locomotives, rolling stock, rail and sleepers for use on Continental railways. Railway works were given the task of making armaments. To save labour, line and rolling stock maintenance was curtailed and liveries simplified.

On the outbreak of the First World War, the government assumed control of the railways under the Railway Executive Committee, consisting of all the managers of the main railway companies; in fact they were well prepared for war and had set up the Railway Executive Committee late in 1912. Nominally it was under the chairmanship of the Board of Trade, but in reality under Herbert Walker, general manager of the London & South Western.

On the declaration of war at midnight on 4/5 August 1914, the War Office gave the Railway Executive Committee sixty hours to collect locomotives and rolling stock to take the British Expeditionary Force to Southampton. Within forty-eight hours it was ready. The British Expeditionary Force landed in France over sixteen days and required 689 special trains, carrying

130,177 men, arms, animals and stores; the busiest day was 22 August, when seventy-three trains were dealt with. The previously prepared movements went just as planned. All this was in addition to the railways' normal day-to-day work.

The Navy also needed supplies, particularly coal, delivered to the Grand Fleet at Scapa Flow. From August 1914 to March 1919, 13,630 coal specials ran from South Wales to Scotland, while naval specials for crews ran nightly in February 1917 between Euston and Thurso, 717 miles in twenty-one and a half hours.

To make room for wartime traffic, some civilian services were curtailed or withdrawn and some stations closed to help alleviate manpower shortage. Some lines, such as Bideford to Westward Ho! and the Basingstoke to Alton, were lifted entirely and the track sent for military use on the Continent.

Some of the best railway officers were lent to the government: Sir Albert Stanley of the Underground was made President of the Board of Trade; Sir Guy Granet of the Midland was appointed Director General of Movements & Railways; Sir Guy Calthrop of the London & North Western became Controller of Mines; Sir Sam Fay of the London & South Western became Controller of Military & Munitions Movements; and Sir Eric Geddes of the North Eastern Railway became Director General of Military Railways and later First Lord of the Admiralty.

Some 49 per cent of railway staff of military age joined the services, some of these being replaced by women who undertook such tasks as being porters, engine cleaners, ticket collectors, shunters and signalwomen, though most lost their jobs after the war as men discharged from the forces were guaranteed re-employment in their previous jobs. When railwaymen joined the forces, many were absorbed into the Railway Operating Division and the Railway Construction Corps where their peacetime skills were valuable. On the outbreak of war, French railways evacuated their locomotives away from the fighting front, so the British Expeditionary Force was required to provide its own engines. Late in 1916 there was a call for 300 locomotives, and by the next year some 675, many from the companies' badly needed stock, had been sent to various fighting fronts.

A standard freight locomotive was required for war service and over 500 Railway Operating Division 2-8-0 engines were built to Robinson's Great Central design.

The Midland & South Western Junction Railway not only served military camps, also carried endless streams of hospital trains from Southampton to the North, old people recounting to the present author that 'them trains never stopped'. Regular runs were made with wounded from Dieppe and Cherbourg, the men still plastered with Flanders mud. In August 1915, extra trains took casualties from the Gallipoli Campaign. Drivers were sometimes so busy that they did not see their families for a fortnight at a time, occasionally working twenty-four hours without rest.

The first Midland & South Western Junction ambulance trains were only allowed one engine and sometimes stalled on a gradient. A doctor told a guard that on one occasion the efforts of the driver to restart had thrown seven men off their stretchers. Two engines were later used, the London & South Western engine arriving at Andover from Southampton being left on and an MSWJR engine coupled in front as pilot. During the war, a total of 1,488 ambulance trains ran over the line. People living beside the railway would hand jugs of tea to troops on the specials. In 1918, when the submarine menace was severe, some of the American troops brought to Liverpool and Glasgow were carried to Southampton by the MSWJR.

The MSWJR locomotive stock needed augmentation for all this wartime traffic and engines belonging to the Great Western, London & South Western and Midland, as well as those of the MSWJR, were shedded at Ludgershall. Once, one of the sidings there held coaches from the Great Central, Great Western, Highland, London & North Western, London & South Western, Midland, North British and North Eastern railways.

Southampton was one of the principal ports for hospital ships and 1,234,248 wounded, requiring 7,822 trains, were dealt with there. After the Battle of the Somme, 1 July 1916, twenty-nine trains departed on 7 July carrying 6,174 wounded and during the weekend of 9 July some 151 trains carried 6,174 disabled soldiers.

The first Canadian troops arrived in thirty-three ships on 15 October 1916, and ninety-two trains were required for transporting them from Plymouth to Salisbury Plain; all were en route to camps by 23 October. There were no less than 176 military camps on the London & South Western and from them an average of 16,500 men travelled on leave each Friday evening or on Saturday, requiring the provision of twenty-one special trains.

The railway factories, in addition to maintaining stock, manufactured war materials; for example, the Great Western at Swindon turned out heavy howitzers and 60-pounder Hotchkiss and anti-aircraft guns, large quantities of medium and heavy calibre shells, bombs, mines and parts for submarines and paravanes. A large quantity of toluol was also produced for use in the manufacture of TNT explosive.

Fortunately, war damage at home was relatively mild: on 16 December 1914, the German cruiser *von der Tann* bombarded coastal towns in the north-east, damaging some railway installations, and both St Pancras and Waterloo suffered in air raids.

January 1917 saw severe restrictions placed on the use of railways, so, except for season tickets, workmen's tickets and traders' concessions, all reduced fares were withdrawn and ordinary fares increased by 50 per cent. Coupled with this, train services were cut and decelerated.

A new port on the south-east coast was found necessary. Richborough was selected and a new railway link made with the South Eastern & Chatham near Minster. Richborough soon had 60 miles of track capable of handling 30,000 tons weekly. In 1917, the Richborough Military Railway had thirty-five locomotives, about 500 wagons, seventeen coaches and dealt with over a million tons. Train ferry berths were constructed at Richborough and Southampton, and on the French side at Dunkirk, Calais, Dieppe and Cherbourg.

As there was a shortage of timber the GWR experimented with concrete sleepers, but many of these failed almost as soon as they were laid. The timber position then improved, and no further experiments were made.

By 1918, Britain's locomotives, rolling stock and permanent way needed much attention, as they had not received sufficient maintenance during the war due to the shortage of manpower. But the war had changed the world. The main British industries of coal, iron, cotton and railway building were less important in the world economy as the importance of oil, hydro-electricity, road transport and light engineering grew. The railways were being seriously challenged by road transport, both the motor lorry and the motor bus, this reducing their income at a time when they needed it increased.

In the post-war world, railwaymen demanded higher pay and were peeved that locomotive crews alone had been given a rise. A strike was called on 26 September 1919, which lasted nine days.

The public was not sympathetic and even those whose names appeared in *Debrett's Peerage* volunteered for manual work. The armed forces protected all stations, bridges and signal boxes. A satisfactory agreement terminated the strike.

The 1921 Railways Act brought in amalgamation on 1 January 1923, whereby the many main railway companies were reduced to the Big Four: the Great Western Railway, the London & North Eastern Railway, the London, Midland & Scottish Railway and the Southern Railway.

The Great Western Railway was the company least affected by Grouping. It was the only one to retain its name and was enlarged by taking over most of the lines in Mid and South Wales, plus the Midland & South Western Junction. As they went through the works for overhaul, many of the pre-Grouping engines were Great Westernised by being fitted with standard Great Western boilers and fittings.

The enlarged company continued the practice of appointing chief officers through internal promotion, which gave a smooth and stable atmosphere. Unfortunately for the company, the South Wales coal industry peaked in 1923 and then suffered a serious decline. Carriage of coal had been an important part of the Great Western economy.

To counteract the high cost of hauling locomotive coal to Devon and Cornwall, relatively far from the coalfields, in 1938 it was proposed that lines west of Taunton would be electrified. This idea was not adopted and the GWR was the only one of the Big Four not to run electric trains. The GWR was the first company to make use of a bus-type diesel engine for rail passenger transport. On 4 December 1933, a streamlined diesel railcar was placed in service in the Reading area. Its interior was typical of contemporary buses and coaches, even to the notice that 'Smokers are requested to occupy rear seats'. Twenty years later, subsequent models were the basis of BR's diesel railcars.

Although in the thirties the GWR ran well-publicised high-speed trains, its attempts at streamlining its locomotives were half-hearted, which was just as well because streamlining on locomotives was only for the modern appearance rather for any benefit in speed.

The London & North Eastern Railway, or the 'London & Nearly Everywhere Railway', was the second largest of the Grouping companies, extending into Scotland and a part of Wales. It comprised the Great Eastern, the Great Central, the Great Northern, the Great North of Scotland, the North British and North Eastern Railways. It relied to a large extent on freight, and, due to the depression in the mining and heavy steel industries, it had the weakest finances of the Big Four. Economies were made and staff employed fell from 207,500 in 1924 to 175,800 in 1937, despite more train miles being worked.

To counteract the growing tonnage lost to roads, fast overnight services were operated between major centres and mechanised marshalling yards opened. The chief mechanical engineer, Nigel Gresley, specialised in building powerful, fast locomotives and in 1938 captured the world speed record for steam, 126 mph. Apart from the non-stop Flying Scotsman, there was the novel luxury cruise train, the Northern Belle.

The intensive London suburban passenger service offered the maximum number of seats in a set train length by Gresley's use of articulation, whereby adjacent carriages shared a bogie. Unlike the other members of the Big Four, the LNER was not interested in the development of air services.

The London, Midland & Scottish Railway was the largest of the Big Four. It comprised the Caledonian Railway, the

Glasgow & South Western, the Highland, the London & North Western, including the Lancashire & Yorkshire with which it had amalgamated in 1922 and the Midland Railway, plus a number of smaller lines including some in Ireland. Together with the Southern Railway it owned the Somerset & Dorset Joint Railway, which gave it access to Bournemouth, which was hardly London and certainly not Midland or Scottish!

The LMS was initially an unhappy railway due to internal strife caused between officers and men of the former London & North Western and those of the Midland Railway, each of whom believed their method was the best.

The adoption of the Midland's centralised train control system was a sensible move, but the adoption of the Midland's small engine policy was poor. In 1926, the general manager and officers' committee was replaced by Sir Josiah Stamp and an executive. This powerful team set about combining of functions and standardisation. The chief mechanical engineer, Sir Henry Fowler, was ordered to produce a more powerful passenger locomotive and the Royal Scot 4-6-0s were the result. Following Fowler's retirement, Stamp appointed William Stanier from the GWR, and Stanier being an outsider meant that the internecine quarrelling between the factions ceased. By 1938, Stanier had reduced the number of locomotive types from 404 to 132. He constructed very comfortable coaches and in 1937 the streamlined Coronation Scot train appeared. His Class 8 2-8-0s were a great improvement on the ex-Midland 0-6-0s, which had continued to be built in the LMS era. Unlike the other Big Four companies, it made little effort at modernising stations.

The Southern Railway was the smallest of the Big Four, its main constituents being the London & South Western, the London, Brighton & South Coast and the South Eastern &

Chatham railways. It had no less than seven London termini – far more than any other company. Apart from the Kent coalfield and quarries, little mineral traffic originated on its system and there was little heavy engineering, thus it relied on passengers for three-quarters of its receipts.

The SR was exceptionally keen on punctuality, and at many stations platform gates were locked just prior to departure to avoid any last-minute delay. Regular interval services meant that passengers did not have to keep referring to a timetable. Shipping played an important part in the company, as, in addition to the ordinary cross-channel services from several south coast ports, there was a train ferry for passenger and goods vehicles. The SR continued the work of developing Southampton as a major port for liners.

Whether or not it was a wise move to construct thirty Merchant Navy class 4-6-2s of radical design and as many as 109 light Pacifics in the 1940s is open to debate; certainly some of the latter seemed to spend much of their time hauling three-coach trains. The coal consumption of these Bulleid Pacifics was heavy and the air-smoothed casing made internal parts difficult to reach. Although the Southern Region, as it became, was the BR region with the greatest area of electrification, it was the last region to employ steam engines on fast expresses.

Railwaymen took part in the General Strike of 1926, sympathetically siding with the miners. Again the public offered assistance, and only a few mishaps were caused by amateurs. The strike lasted eight days and when the railwaymen returned they had to sign a form relinquishing their previous rights to permanency of employment. Many refused, and the railway companies yielded. Some were better off financially because of the strike. Strike pay offered by the Railway Clerks' Association was £1 15s per week per man, whereas a man aged twenty earned only £1 8s a week, so during the strike he was seven shillings better off. Most men were not; they were normally paid £3 16s.

The strike seriously harmed the railways as it showed many the advantages of road transport, passengers turning to buses, coaches or private cars while industry turned to lorries. The strike was a short-sighted move, as the railways no longer held a transport monopoly. The LMS found that between 1923 and 1927 buses had creamed off 27 per cent of receipts of journeys up to 10 miles, while motor lorries took the profitable traffic in high-value goods and left the railways to carry the less profitable. By the end of 1928, the railways had acquired the power to own, or have financial interest in, road transport concerns. The railways took a controlling interest in many bus and coach companies, particularly in the Tilling and British Electric Traction groups, while by August 1933 they acquired a controlling interest in the road haulage firms Carter Paterson and Pickfords.

The period had four great locomotive engineers – Churchward, Collett, Stanier and Gresley. George Jackson Churchward, a bachelor, dedicated his life to the development of the steam engine. He began as an apprentice at the South Devon Railway works, Newton Abbot, in 1873. From his early days he envisaged standard types of engines that bore the maximum interchangeability of components and made the most efficient use of steam generated. Churchward had knowledge of engines in the United States which were practical and strongly made and also those in France, where maximum thermal efficiency was sought. When he took charge of design at Swindon in 1902 he produced a stud of engines second to none, and his engines – and those of his successor, Charles Benjamin Collett, who followed his principles – provided power for express passenger and heavy freight until the abolition of steam on BR's Western Region in 1965. One of Churchward's assistants, William Stanier, became chief mechanical engineer of the London, Midland & Scottish Railway and produced very efficient engines, while he, in turn, had Robert Riddles, Ernest Stewart Cox and Roland Bond as assistants and this trio produced British Railways' Standard class locomotives, including the amazing Class 9F 2-10-0s, which, although freight locomotives, ran freely on express passenger trains up to 90 mph.

Churchward favoured high-pressure boilers, superheaters, long-travel, long-lap valves and large axle-box-bearing surfaces and these combined elements produced exceptionally efficient and reliable locomotives. Some of Churchward's early engines were ungainly, and an assistant, Harry Holcroft, smoothed their appearance.

Although Churchward designed the 4-6-2 *The Great Bear*, it proved to be something of a white elephant as it was too heavy for most of the Great Western main lines and the traffic department was quite content with his two-cylinder Saints and four-cylinder Stars, as it was later with Collett's four-cylinder Castles and Kings. Unfortunately, Churchward was no sentimentalist and scrapped two historic broad gauge locomotives – *North Star*, built in 1837, and *Lord of the Isles* of 1851 – because they took up workshop space which he required for new engines.

When the LNER was formed, the board of directors offered the post of chief mechanical engineer to the most senior from among the constituent companies. This was John George Robinson of the Great Central Railway, who had designed excellent locomotives including the 2-8-0 class chosen by the Railway Operating Division of the Royal Engineers in the First World War. Feeling too old at sixty-seven, he suggested that the board appoint Nigel Gresley of the Great Northern, who accepted the post.

In 1924, the LNER exhibited Gresley's A1 class Pacific No. 4472 *Flying Scotsman* alongside the GWR's 4-6-0 No. 4073 *Caerphilly Castle*; their dimensions differed:

|  | *Flying Scotsman* | *Caerphilly Castle* |
|---|---|---|
| Weight | 92 tons | 80 tons |
| Length | 70 feet | 65 feet |
| Grate area | 41.25 sq. feet | 29.36 sq. feet |
| Heating surface | 2,930 sq. feet | 1,963 sq. feet |
| Tractive effort | 29,835 lb | 31,625 lb |

Tractive effort is determined by calculating the square of the diameter of the piston, multiplied by the piston stroke, multiplied by 85 per cent of the maximum boiler pressure, divided by double the diameter of the driving wheels. For two-cylinder engines, which most locomotives are, this is the final figure, but if a three-cylinder machine the result should be increased by 50 per cent, or 100 per cent for four cylinders.

Stephenson's *Rocket* had a tractive effort of 820 lb, and the broad gauge *Iron Duke* one of 8,262 lb.

Tractive effort shows the pulling force available on starting a train and is only a rough-and-ready means of comparing locomotives. For instance, a machine with an inadequate boiler may have a high tractive effort, but then run out of steam soon after it moves; or a small firebox may not produce enough heat to provide sufficient steam.

Seeing *Flying Scotsman* and *Caerphilly Castle* side by side, it appeared that the former looked to be more powerful; yet tractive effort figures said otherwise.

In late April 1925, the LNER's No. 4474 *Victor Wild* (the same class as *Flying Scotsman*) and No. 4074 *Caldicot Castle* ran on trials. *Victor Wild*, with its LNER crew, was able to handle the Cornish Riviera Limited successfully, but *Caldicot Castle* knocked fifteen minutes off the time allowed and even used 6 lb less coal per mile, making a saving of more than half a ton from Paddington to Plymouth. Part of the increased coal consumption of *Victor Wild* was due to its longer wheelbase necessitating downhill speeds to be restricted. Following the trials, the GWR improved its curves and Gresley improved his Pacifics.

Much the same thing happened when No. 4073 *Caerphilly Castle* hauled LNER expresses, burning 6 per cent less coal than No. 2545 *Diamond Jubilee* running on its home territory. Although Gresley appeared to have built a more powerful engine, Churchward understood more about valve design, which allowed steam-free entrance and exit from the cylinders. The result was the appearance in 1928 of Gresley's efficient A3 class Pacifics and the suitable modification of his A1 class.

It was not surprising that one of his 'race horse' Pacifics, No. 4479, was named *Robert the Devil*, as this was the nickname of William the Conqueror's father, to whom Gresley's ancestors were related. No quite so appropriate was the occasion when *Robert the Devil* was rostered to haul a special train for the Methodist Church Conference!

On 1 May 1928, the LNER introduced a non-stop train between London and Edinburgh.

Called the Flying Scotsman, it was headed by No. 4472 *Flying Scotsman*. Covering a distance of 393 miles, it was the world's longest regular non-stop run. As the distance would have been too great for the responsibility of one crew, Gresley devised a corridor tender with a gap 1½ feet wide and 5 feet high, through which a relief crew could squeeze after riding 'on the cushions' in a compartment of the leading coach. Gresley discovered the minimum width required in a practical way by lining up chairs along his dining room wall and squeezing by. Ten tenders were constructed that year for the A1 class Pacifics – they later became A3 class after rebuilding – and corridor tenders were also attached to the streamlined A4 class.

On 1 May 1928, the engine of the first Up Flying Scotsman bore a headboard prepared by the Edinburgh Haymarket shed in the style of that used on their local trains. On arrival of the Flying Scotsman at King's Cross, the authorities there prepared a similar headboard. This was the start of the Big Four using headboards on their principal expresses.

Officials of the LNER were very practical. Between 1924 and 1927, when new first-class sleeping cars were being built, Oliver Bulleid entered N. Newsome's office and asked him how he prepared to retire for the night. Newsome explained that he removed his jacket and waistcoat, placing them on the bed until after he had hung his trousers on a hanger. Bulleid observed that a hanger should be designed so that the garments could be hung in the proper sequence. Thus a horizontal trouser support was placed above, instead of below the curved portion for the jacket.

In 1925, Gresley introduced his P1 class 2-8-2 goods engines, designed to draw hundred-wagon coal trains. A striking feature was an auxiliary booster engine on the trailing axle, brought into use to assist starting or climbing a stiff gradient. Using the booster, the starting effort was 47,000 lb. With 5-foot-2-inch driving wheels, they were mixed-traffic engines, suitable for either goods or passenger work. The engine was really a little before its time as the existing loops were too short to hold hundred-wagon trains to enable faster trains to overtake.

Nine years later, Gresley produced his P2 class of 2-8-2, with a tractive effort of 43,462 lb. They were designed to draw heavy sleeping-car expresses between Edinburgh and Aberdeen. Smoke deflectors were essential as the large boiler only allowed space within the loading gauge for a short chimney, and were required to prevent drifting steam obscuring a driver's view. Rather than being bolted on, the deflectors were a forward projection of the boiler casing. Drivers liked the engines, which carried out the duties required of them very effectively, but firemen were not so enamoured as they consumed more coal than Pacifics for doing the same work. In 1943–44, Gresley's successor, Edward Thompson rebuilt them into very mundane Pacifics. At the time of writing, a group of enthusiasts are making a new-build P2.

N. L. R. Return
Available day of Issue or
from Saturday to Monday
HIGHBURY
TO
BROAD STREET
5d 2nd Class
Not transferable
Issued subject to the
Company's Published
Regulations.

54194

N. L. R. Return
Available day of Is
or following day or fr
Saturday to Monday
BOW
TO
BROAD STREE
6d 2nd. Cls
Not transferable
Issued subject to
Company's Public
Regulations.

4383

DISTRICT RAILWAY
Available for day of issue only.
WESTMINSTER BRIDGE
N          TO          Series 26
EDGWARE ROAD
VIA BAYSWATER
THIRD CLASS FARE 4D

8716          8716

# 12

# Speed in the 1930s

In 1923, the GWR decided to claim the fastest train in Britain, which hitherto had been held by the LNER with a forty-three-minute run over the 44.1 miles from Darlington to York. The Up Cheltenham Flyer was to make the 77.3 miles from Swindon to Paddington in seventy-five minutes, an average of 61.8 mph. Timing of the train was gradually decreased, and in September 1932 was cut to sixty-five minutes, requiring a start-to-stop average of 71.4 mph. Its best run was on 6 June 1932, when the journey was covered in fifty-six minutes and forty-seven seconds at an average speed of 81.5 mph.

In 1933 the Germans introduced the diesel-powered Flying Hamburger, which ran for a great distance at 100 mph. Gresley believed that steam traction could equal this and furthermore offer greater seating accommodation as well as dining facilities. He asked the manufacturers of the German diesel train to estimate the time required for one of their sets to speed the 185.7 miles from King's Cross to Leeds; the answer was 165 minutes.

No. 4472 *Flying Scotsman* reached Leeds in 151 minutes 16 seconds. Returning to London with two extra coaches added, she raced down Stoke Bank at 100 mph and reached London in 157 minutes. On 5 March 1935, a similar train cut the proposed

German schedule to Newcastle by eighteen minutes and on its return averaged 100.2 mph for 12¼ miles.

Gresley then designed the A4 Pacifics with a streamlined casing especially for high-speed work, and the design was swift too. The frames of No. 2509 *Silver Link* were laid on 26 June 1935 and the engines emerged from the Doncaster works on 7 September.

At a press run on 27 September, 110 years to the day from when George Stephenson drove *Locomotion No 1*, she reached 112.5 mph and averaged 100 mph for 43 miles; that is, not far short of today's speeds. On a trial run with a train full of railway officials and reporters, there was a terrifying 'thrump' as the train hit the curve south of Hatfield station at 97 mph, and someone remarked that a crash then would result in considerable promotion among the LNER and newspaper staffs. Passengers travelling on the streamlined Silver Jubilee with its special coaches were required to pay a supplement of five shillings, and this repaid the building cost of the train within two years. When the regulator of an A4 was opened fully, steam flowed into the cylinders at virtually the same pressure as it left the boiler – Gresley had certainly learned his lesson. The Silver Jubilee, with its two-tone silver-and-grey livery, was highly popular and profitable, earning thirteen shillings a mile net, which was about double that of a conventional express.

In July 1937, the year of King George VI's coronation, a new streamlined express, air-conditioned and with a beaver-tailed observation car at its rear, was introduced between London and Edinburgh to cover the 393 miles in six hours, representing an average speed of 71.9 mph. Then, on 3 July 1938, during high-speed brake tests, No. 4468 *Mallard* (named after Gresley's favourite bird at his moated house near St Albans) attained a momentary speed of 126 mph down Stoke Bank – a world record for steam traction. *Mallard* had a double Kylchap exhaust, which provided a strong and uniform exhaust across all of the boiler tubes in the smoke box, thus improving combustion while decreasing cylinder back-pressure. During the Second World War, an A4 heading a twenty-one-coach Flying Scotsman ran between Darlington and York at an average speed of 76 mph. Unfortunately, subsequent locomotive engineers did not maintain the pace of steam development demonstrated by Gresley.

His Pacific *Dominion of Canada* was fitted with a Canadian Pacific Railway whistle and also a CPR bell. One enthusiastic driver put it to such good use that, one day, passing through a Hertfordshire station, the fire brigade turned out. The LNER then wisely rendered the bell inoperative.

Gresley had one failure – No. 10000, a 4-6-4 which appeared in 1929. Its main feature was a water-tube boiler, a type which had been found economical and was used in factories, power stations and ships. Instead of heat passing through tubes in the boiler as in a conventional locomotive, heat was converted into steam in banks of tubes linking lower and upper water drums. Its advantage was that it could work at a far higher pressure, making it far more efficient. Gresley's problem was fitting a water-tube boiler within the British loading gauge.

Gresley's water-tube compound engine, with a boiler pressure of 450 lb/sq. inch, compared with the 200 to 250 lb of other express engines, was intended to be a more efficient version of the Flying Scotsman A1s. No. 10000's problem of poor steaming was overcome by using a double Kylchap exhaust, but the main drawback to the design was that maintenance costs were appreciably higher than for a standard Pacific. With the very efficient A4s appearing in 1935, it was withdrawn in 1936.

An interesting concept patented in 1917 by William Joseph Still was a steam-diesel hybrid, a reciprocating engine with double-acting cylinders, the top half diesel and the bottom half steam. When starting, steam was supplied from an oil-fed boiler, but when running, steam was generated by the diesel exhaust, allowing steam to boost the diesel cylinders.

In 1926, Kitson & Company of Leeds built a 2-6-2T for testing on the LNER. It started with steam, diesel power cutting in at 5 mph. Maximum power provided by the diesel was 800 hp, with a further 200 hp provided by steam. Fuel consumption was good, but the machine was no match for Gresley's steam engines and the Kitson-Still, although not unsuccessful, was broken up by the Kitson company in 1935.

On 15 June 1928, a contest to Scotland was arranged between a train and plane. Although not strictly a race, the simultaneous working of a flight and a non-stop rail journey between London and Edinburgh was seen as a means of direct comparison between the two modes of transport and was made in the full glare of publicity.

In order that the train could be identified from the air, one of the coaches had 'Flying Scotsman' painted on the roof. The day began with breakfast for about fifty passengers at London's Savoy Hotel. All the airborne party of twenty-one was present, together with a small fraction of the 300 train passengers who had booked seats in advance. The fliers included the Director of Civil Aviation, Air Vice-Marshall Sir William Sefton Brancker, and James Birkett, a seventy-nine-year-old former LNER driver who was to assist the pilot, Captain Gordon P. Olley, in identifying the train.

Both aircraft and train passengers left the Savoy Hotel together. Although the plane, the Armstrong-Whitworth Argosy biplane *City of Glasgow*, with its top speed of 115 mph, flew faster, it had to stop twice to refuel. When the Flying Scotsman arrived at

Waverley eleven minutes early it was declared the winner, the air passengers coming from Edinburgh's Turnhouse airport having been delayed by traffic and not appearing until four minutes after the train's arrival.

Another leading locomotive engineer of the thirties was William Stanier, Collett's deputy. When offered the post of chief mechanical engineer of the London, Midland & Scottish Railway in 1932, he accepted. When the LMS was formed in the 1923 amalgamation, it was restricted by J. E. Anderson's dogma that small engines should be the norm and that if one could not cope then another should be hung on the front.

Stanier's first important LMS engine was a two-cylinder Class 5 mixed-traffic 4-6-0. A development of the GWR Hall class, they were free-steaming and could reach 96 mph, yet could also be at home on goods trains. His Class 8F 2-8-0s were designed for heavy freight work. Some of Stanier's early designs were not very efficient. This was because conditions on the LMS were different from those on the GWR; when given higher superheating, the Class 5s used 12 per cent less coal and 14 per cent less water for doing the same work. His Jubilee class 4-6-0 could be considered a three-cylinder express version of his Class 5.

The Princess Royal class of 1933 was closely modelled on the GWR *The Great Bear* and the King class. On 16 November 1936, a member of the class, 4-6-2 No. 6201 *Princess Elizabeth*, with an enlarged superheater, made a non-stop 401-mile run Euston to Glasgow in five hours and fifty-three minutes, at an average speed of 68.2 mph, with one crew throughout as no corridor tender was provided. The following day, with eight coaches instead of seven, she returned in five hours and forty-four minutes at an average speed of 70.15 mph – taking not much longer than today's Pendolinos.

In 1935 he produced the Class 8 2-8-0, a modernised GWR 28XX class, and the same year brought out his version of Fowler's 2-6-2T and 2-6-4Ts. The year 1937 saw the appearance of an improved Princess Royal, the streamlined Princess Coronation class, and No. 6220 *Coronation* reached a speed of 114 mph. His rebuilt Royal Scots were probably the finest 4-6-0 in Britain.

It was believed that the 2,000 hp 90 mph diesel-electrics in service from 1958 would be able to do the work of the 3,000 ihp, 100 mph-plus Stanier Pacifics on the West Coast route. Although the Pacifics were faster, diesels had more rapid acceleration up to about 30 mph and this feature was important where delays could be frequent and the ability to accelerate rapidly useful. Management believed 4,000 lb of coal per hour to be the maximum for hand firing. Though the sustained maximum power of a Coronation class with a 50-foot-square grate could have been increased with a mechanical stoker, the authorities were reluctant to introduce them as the initial cost was higher, maintenance costs were higher and fuel consumption would have been increased by about 25 per cent. A point overlooked was that steam engines could run faster when required to regain time. If fitted with mechanical stokers, the Coronation Pacifics could have matched the timings demanded when the line was electrified and cleared for 100 mph running in 1965.

Although most of Stanier's engines were conventional, he experimented with a turbine-driven Princess Royal Pacific, No. 6202, known as the Turbomotive, which proved efficient and marginally more frugal in water and coal consumption compared with her four-cylinder sisters. She was smoother running and gave less hammer blow – the thrust of the connecting rod on the crank, transmitted through the driving wheels to the rail. A driver could vary the power output by selecting between one and six nozzles blasting steam on the turbine. A reverse turbine was selected by a clutch. The main drawback was that, as she was a one-off, spare parts were not readily available; indeed, she was out of service for periods awaiting them. She was withdrawn in 1949 and emerged on 15 August 1952 as an ordinary four-cylinder Pacific, but unfortunately was destroyed in the Harrow & Wealdstone disaster of 8 October that year.

The 1930s was an era of modernisation: the GWR streamlined *King Henry VII* and *Manorbier Castle* and introduced a 'shirt button' emblem. The SR adopted 'clock face' timetables, and its system received a modern image with the adoption of bright yellow 'sunshine' lettering with a halo outline.

With the formation of British Railways in 1948, Robert Riddles believed that, with no capital available for electrification, steam was the way forward as the country had plenty of coal and water whereas oil had to be imported. The initial cost of steam was cheaper: a BR Standard Class 5 cost £16,000, whereas an equivalent diesel-electric was £78,200, while repair costs for steam were only about a third of that for diesels. Riddles and his team believed that steam should ultimately give way to electric traction. Another member of the team, Roland Bond, expected main-line steam to be extinct by 1985, or 1995 at the latest. The BR Standard locomotives were not an advance in design, they were just competent engines with labour-saving rocking grates and hopper ash pans. With only two cylinders, one of the main objects of the design was to render all working parts to have easy access. Arguably the best Standard locomotives were the 2-10-0 Class 9s, costing £23,975. Although primarily designed for heavy freight, they proved excellent mixed-traffic engines and could haul express passenger trains up to 90 mph. Perhaps their cheapness was one of the reasons for the briefness of their reign – had they been expensive like a diesel, it would have seemed wasteful to write them off prematurely.

The only truly express passenger locomotive built by BR was the solitary three-cylinder No. 71000 *Duke of Gloucester*. Completed in 1954, with improved Caprotti valve-gear cylinder, its performance was highly efficient, but it steamed indifferently and was disliked by crews used to Coronations. Manufacturing faults have been corrected in preservation, vastly improving performance.

Oliver Bulleid, when he moved from the LNER to the Southern Railway, produced some startling locomotives. His aim was for an engine to pull 600-ton trains at 70 mph. He designed the Merchant Navy class Pacific but, with the war on, construction of new locomotives required government sanction as engineering efforts had to be geared towards the needs of war. Because they had 6-foot-2-inch driving wheels, he was just able to claim that they were mixed-traffic engines.

Of surprising appearance, the first, 21C-1 *Channel Packet*, appeared in 1941 with an air-smoothed casing and the wheels disc-type rather than spoked. It was revolutionary: the chain-driven valve gear was enclosed in an oil bath, lighting was electric and not oil; the firebox was steel, not copper. The Merchant Navy class proved to be powerful and fast. As with many new things, it was not without its faults. The oil bath tended to leak and the lubricant ran on to the rails and caused slipping and occasionally fire; the steam reverser suffered steam leakage and could move from 25 per cent cut-off to 75 per cent accidentally.

In addition to the thirty engines of the Merchant Navy class, between 1945 and 1951 no less than 109 lightweight versions were built. Known as the West Country and Battle of Britain classes, they were useful as they provided plenty of power on lines which were not strong enough for a Merchant Navy, though the number built could be criticised as many light Pacifics spent much of their time hauling two-coach trains which could have been adequately handled by a smaller and cheaper engine.

In 1956, Merchant Navy No. 35018 *British India Line* was rebuilt with the air-smoothed casing, chain drive, oil bath and steam reverser removed. It proved a fine and much-improved engine. All the class were converted and work started on their lightweight sisters, but then in 1961, with about half the class still to convert, British Railways believed no more money should be invested in steam. During the last days of steam on the Southern Region the Merchant Navy Pacifics often reached 100 mph or more.

Bulleid's second engine type appeared in 1942. His Q1 class 0-6-0 was as startling in appearance as a Merchant Navy. It was indeed an austerity engine with no frills. The boiler cladding did not give a smooth outline and it lacked a running board and splashers over the driving wheels. Weighing only 51¼ tons, it was the most powerful British 0-6-0 and capable of running up to 75 mph.

In 1949, he produced what probably represented a step too far: the 0-6-6-0 Leader class. With a driving cab at both ends, and looking similar to a diesel-electric, the central cab for the fireman was completely closed and became far too hot. Another important failure was to provide adequate steam. Only one machine was completed.

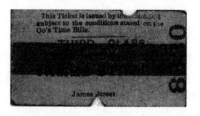

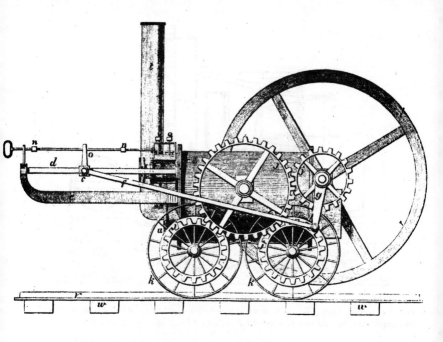

121. Probable design of Trevithick's first locomotive, built in 1804. (Author's collection)

122. A drawing by Thomas Rowlandson of the temporary track near the site of the later Euston station, on which Trevithick's locomotive *Catch Me Who Can* ran in 1808. (Author's collection)

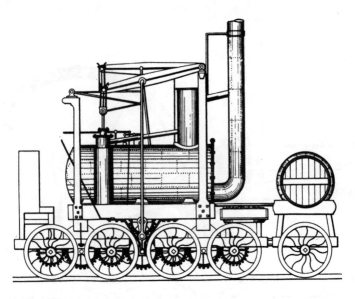

123. The multi-wheeled Wylam colliery locomotive around 1814, when altered to spread its weight over the cast-iron rails in order to prevent breakage. (Author's collection)

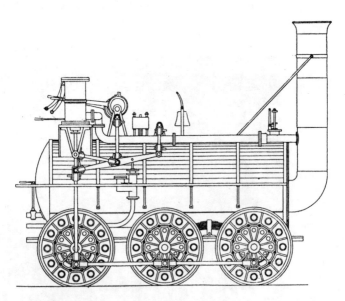

124. Timothy Hackworth's drawing of the *Royal George*, built in 1827. (Author's collection)

Mechanics' Magazine,

MUSEUM, REGISTER, JOURNAL, AND GAZETTE.

No. 324.]        SATURDAY, OCTOBER 24, 1829.        [Price 3d.

"THE ROCKET," LOCOMOTIVE STEAM ENGINE OF
MR. ROBERT STEPHENSON.

125. The earliest known contemporary illustration of Stephenson's *Rocket*. (Author's collection)

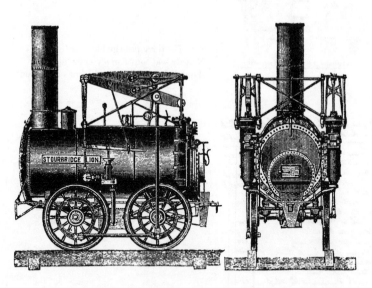

126. The *Stourbridge Lion*, built by Foster, Rastrick & Co., 1829. (Author's collection)

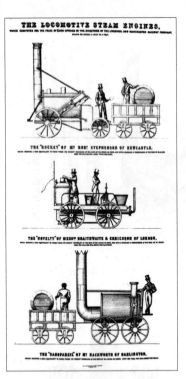

127. The three principal locomotives *Rocket, Novelty* and *Sans Pareil* competing in the Rainhill Trials of 1829. (Author's collection)

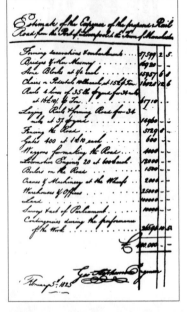

128. The estimated cost of building the Liverpool & Manchester Railway, signed by George Stephenson. (Author's collection)

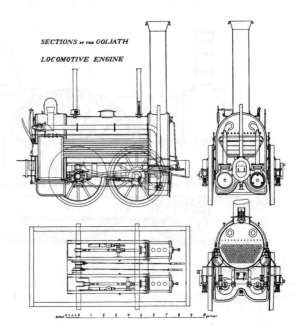

SECTIONS *of the* GOLIATH

LOCOMOTIVE ENGINE

SCALE

129. Sections of Robert Stephenson's *Goliath* around March 1831. (Author's collection)

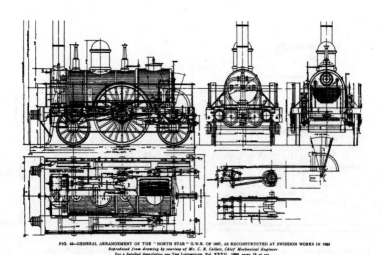

FIG. 43—GENERAL ARRANGEMENT OF THE " NORTH STAR " G.W.R. OF 1837, AS RECONSTRUCTED AT SWINDON WORKS IN 1925
*Reproduced from drawing by courtesy of Mr. C. B. Collett, Chief Mechanical Engineer*
For a detailed description see THE LOCOMOTIVE, Vol. XXXII., 1926, page 16 *et seq.*

130. The general arrangement of the GWR *North Star* of 1837, as reconstructed at Swindon works in 1925. (Author's collection)

131. Due to limitations brought about by Brunel's requirements, early GWR engines were unsuccessful, those built by Matthew Dixon & Co. in 1838 being withdrawn in 1840. These 'boat' engines had 10-foot-diameter driving wheels. (Author's collection)

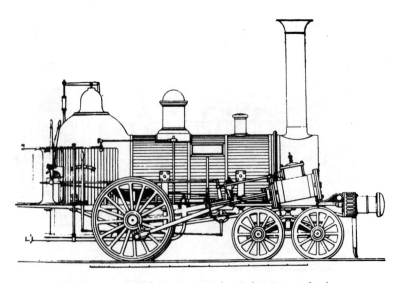

132. An American type 4-2-0 built by Benjamin Hick at Bolton in 1840 for the Birmingham & Gloucester Railway. (Author's collection)

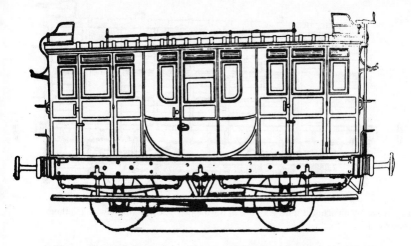

133. First- and second-class coach with a guard's seat at each end and with railed top for luggage. The centre compartment owes much to stagecoach design. It was built around 1841 by Atkinson & Philipson for the Edinburgh & Northern Railway. (Author's collection)

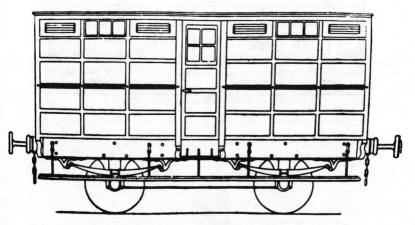

134. A covered Parliamentary class coach with only one door each side. Seated passengers could not see out. Built by Atkinson & Philipson in 1844. (Author's collection)

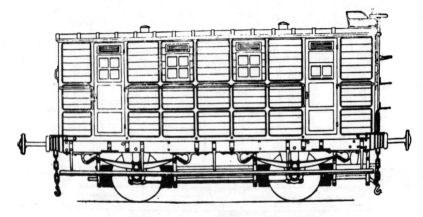

135. A four-compartment third-class coach for the Leeds & Thirsk Railway. (Author's collection)

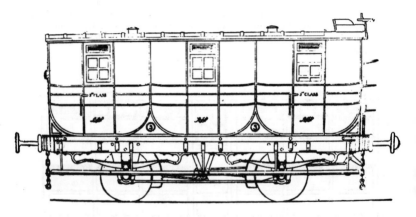

136. A three-compartment third-class coach with guard's seat built in 1847 for the Leeds & Thirsk Railway. (Author's collection)

137. In 1847, William Knee of Bristol designed a roll-on roll-off pantechnicon. It is on a broad gauge wagon. (Author's collection)

Between **LONDON** and **EPSOM**.

SECOND CLASS.

No. 35.L.                                    11th April 1849

Pass Mr. William Tibb

For **TWELVE** Months to expire on the

Tenth day of April 18

(Signature) W Tibb                          By order J. Buckler
                                                         SECRETARY.

Received 10s., to be returned if this Ticket is delivered up at the date of Expiry.

138. A second-class annual season ticket issued 10 April 1850 for use between London and Epsom. (Author's collection)

ERECTING SHED.

139. The erecting shed at Swindon in 1852: the 4-2-2 *Swallow* built in 1849, left, and 0-6-0 *Hero*, built in 1851, right. (Author's collection)

140. The 2-2-2 *Jenny Lind*, built by E. B. Wilson in 1847 for the London & North Western Railway. (Author's collection)

141. An 1848 engraving of a Crampton 4-2-0. As the driving wheels were placed behind the firebox, this design offered the advantage of a low centre of gravity. (Author's collection)

142. Engraving of the Armagh runaway on the Great Northern Railway of Ireland, 12 June 1889. (Author's collection)

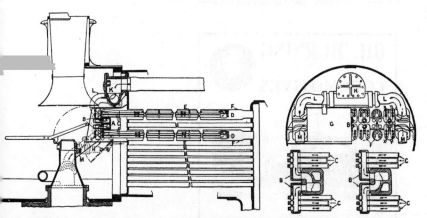

The Swindon Superheater, 1912. Main header A connects with fingers B carrying tubes C whose ends are coupled in pairs to bends D. Plates E support the tubes C in the large flues F. Hinged plate G encloses the header in the smokebox, and the lower flap H is a damper, automatically opened when the regulator K is opened. Steam then passes along L to the top chamber of header A, to one finger B, through tubes C and back via second finger B to the lower chamber of header A, thence through pipe M to the cylinders.

143. The Swindon superheater, 1912. (Author's collection)

144. Advertisement for the Highland Railway's hotel at Inverness. (Author's collection)

145. An advertisement in the *Railway Year Book 1922* for the Scarab oil-burning system. (Author's collection)

# 13

# The Second World War

As the Second World War seemed inevitable, the Railway Executive Committee was formed on 24 September 1938. Its chairman was Sir Ralph Wedgwood of the LNER (interestingly, second cousin of the composer Ralph Vaughan Williams), with his deputy Sir James Milne of the GWR, other members being Sir William Wood of the London, Midland & Scottish; Gilbert Szlumper of the Southern; and Frank Pick of the London Passenger Transport Board. The Railway Executive Committee's headquarters was in Down Street station on the Piccadilly line between Green Park and Hyde Park Corner stations. The platforms at Down Street were walled off from the tracks and made soundproof to form offices, kitchen, mess rooms and dormitories. As it was deep below the surface, it could not be penetrated by a bomb.

Plans were prepared for mobilising troops, evacuating cities, taking air-aid precautions, working under blackout conditions, bringing privately owned wagons under common usage and providing ambulance trains.

The Military Training Act of 26 May 1939 required all railwaymen aged twenty to twenty-one to register for National Service. The railway companies asked for their employees to be declared to be in a 'reserved occupation'. For most clerical grades this meant that those aged over twenty-five were exempt, but for the more manual workers it was thirty. Railways lost about 100,000 men to National Service in the Second World War compared with 185,000 in the First World War.

By July 1939, the evacuation of children from eighteen vulnerable zones was organised. Under the Emergency Powers Defence Act of 1939, the Minister of Transport had powers to take over the country's railways. When he took control on 1 September 1939, he appointed R. H. Hill as control officer and an intermediary between the ministry and the Railway Executive Committee.

A great evacuation of children was ordered on 31 August 1939 as serious bombing was expected. Between 1 and 4 of September, some 1,334,358 persons were evacuated in 3,823 trains. They included 617,480 from the London area, 161,879 from Liverpool and Birkenhead, 123, 639 from Glasgow and Clydebank and 115, 779 from Manchester and Salford. Each child wore a label with its name, address, party number and medical symbols. To prevent accidents, doors of compartments containing only children were locked.

Then came the Phoney War – and thus no bombing – so many of the evacuees drifted back to their homes. However, with the invasion of Holland, Belgium and France in May 1940, another evacuation was organised.

The evacuation of 319,000 troops from Dunkirk between 27 May and 4 June 1940 required 620 trains from Dover. Then, at the end of the first week of June 1940, the 320,000 evacuated men were taken from reception centres to camps for re-equipment and rehabilitation, while concurrently 200 trains were run from south-western ports, principally Plymouth, to transport men evacuated from the Bay of Biscay area. As one of the German intelligence centres was believed to be Dublin, between 16 and 19 June, twenty-three trains carried a defence force to Northern Ireland via Stranraer.

Railways set up Local Defence Volunteer Corps, later to become the Home Guard, to protect vulnerable railway facilities such as goods yards, tunnels, bridges and viaducts. Initially armed with golf clubs, shunting poles and pick-axe handles, they watched for saboteurs or parachute invaders. Later they were supplied with guns, and ammunition, while others manned anti-aircraft batteries near marshalling yards and major stations. More than 156,000 railwaymen joined the Home Guard.

In the event of an air raid, on receipt of a Red warning, passenger trains were required to stop at the first station, allow any passengers who wished to step out to do so, and then proceed at not more than 15 mph. Goods trains were required to stop at the first signal box to receive instructions and then continue not in excess of 10 mph. As there were so many warnings in the summer and autumn of 1940 that rail transport was chaotic, in July an extra warning, Purple, was added to indicate that enemy aircraft were in the vicinity and that all lights should be extinguished. Red now indicated 'imminent danger'. Speed restrictions were eased in November 1940 and only at night were trains stopped and drivers instructed to proceed at not over 30 mph.

Air-raid warnings for railways were sounded after the civil warning, and roof-watch schemes gave a last-minute announcement when raiders were near in order to allow more time for such activities as shunting. Due to the noise of shunting, which could drown an alarm, high-pitched gongs were used which penetrated railway noise. For safety, railway companies' headquarters were dispersed from the capital: the GWR to Aldermaston, Berkshire; the LMS to Watford; the LNER to Hitchin, Hertfordshire; and the SR to Deepdene, Surrey.

There was not always time to stop when a driver spotted a crater ahead. In 1941, seven GWR locomotives were driven into craters. On 28 April 1941, 4-6-0 No. 4936 *Kinlet Hall* fell into a crater between Menheniot and St Germans and the crater was so deep that, though *Kinlet Hall* was only slightly damaged, it took four days to extricate.

Rolling stock was dispersed overnight to safe places – Brighton stock was removed to Kemp Town tunnel; likewise at Dover to the tunnel and at Bath to Bitton.

As the Forth and Tay bridges were so vital for communication, to prevent sabotage, passengers were required to place all their luggage in the guard's van and were only permitted to retain packages too small to contain a bomb.

Deliberate bombing by the enemy did not cause really serious damage, but some of the worst effects were just unlucky chance. On 19 April 1941, a parachute mine destroyed the SR's Southwark Street bridge, severing eight roads, while in May 1943 a bouncing bomb wrecked a pier and two arches of the viaduct at Brighton. When Birmingham New Street signal box, 76 feet long and with a 152-lever frame, was damaged beyond repair, a replacement box was opened just eleven days later.

A German bomber crashed on the roof of Victoria station. The official report read, 'Many important missions have arrived at Victoria, but never before in this fashion.'

In the Second World War, 484 locomotives were damaged and all but eight of these could be repaired, proving the excellent construction of British engines. Some 637 coaches and 2,685 wagons were also destroyed. St Pancras station received heavy bombing and bombs blocked a tunnel near St John's Wood. It was two months before interlaced tracks could be opened, and proper double-line working was not restored until a further nine months had passed. After the Coventry blitz of 14/15 November 1940, except for one remote avoiding line, every rail route in the city was blocked and the station itself unusable, yet working was restored within a week.

Railwaymen could work remarkably quickly. At 12.10 p.m. on 2 October 1943, the SR Exeter Divisional Superintendent received a telephone call from the United States' Army asking for a temporary siding on the Exmouth branch to unload 150 wagons arriving from the North. By 7 October, the sidings, reached by a new embankment, had been laid and the signalling installed. At Lockerley on the Salisbury to Romsey line, the United States' Army Supply Depot required 15 miles of sidings and 134 large sheds concealed among the trees.

To cope with the event of a major route being severed by bombing, new connections were made to enable trains to use an alternative. For example, the GWR and the SR had new links inserted at St Budeaux, Lydford, Launceston and Yeovil, while Thingley Junction near Chippenham became a triangular junction as did Heywood near Westbury. These new connections were made at government expense and were government and not railway property, although they were managed by the relevant company.

In 1943, 150 bomber airfields were being built in East Anglia. Country stations near these sites coped with ten times their normal traffic as trains arrived with building material and rubble from bombed cities. The LNER ran 460 special trains to assemble all the airmen at these new bases, while each 1,000 bomber raids required twenty-eight fuel trains and another eight carrying bombs.

In an attempt to fool German bombers, dummy marshalling yards were set up not far from the genuine article by a team from Sound City Film Studios, Shepperton, Surrey. One such decoy was made near Whitemoor, near March, Cambridgeshire, which had the largest yard in Britain and the second largest in Europe. Others were set up at Stoke Gifford, near Bristol, and Knowsley,

Liverpool. Lights were put in place to illuminate tracks while dummy locomotives had glowing fireboxes.

At the outbreak of war, the speed limit was reduced to 60 mph to help ease maintenance on permanent way and rolling stock. Locomotive liveries were simplified and many became just black, while to maximise space on trains most sleeping and restaurant cars were withdrawn. Express passenger trains became lengthy, sometimes as much as twenty coaches long, and on 31 March 1940, V2 class 2-6-2 No. 4800 hauled a twenty-six-coach train carrying 1,300 passengers from Peterborough to King's Cross and on arrival the last four coaches were still in Gasworks Tunnel. On at least one occasion, a Down express consisted of twenty-five coaches, which meant that the engine and first coach were not only beyond the platform at King's Cross, but well inside Gasworks Tunnel. Lengthy trains meant that at some stations trains had to draw up twice. For example, many GWR express trains consisted of sixteen coaches, but as Bath Spa station could only hold eight it was necessary to draw up again. This could cause problems in the blackout. When a train stopped at Bath, a sailor stepped out on to what in the dark he believed was the platform. Actually, it was the girder of a river bridge. He continued walking and plunged into the river. Fortunately the story did not have a fatal ending, but to avoid a reoccurrence the GWR erected a fence on the girder.

Overcrowding was notorious. The author can remember travelling in a compartment for which there were only eight seats, being packed with sixteen passengers and a baby. Many travellers vowed that when peace came they would buy a car and never use a train again. The coaches on some trains were weighed down so that 'their springs were flattened to a degree which resulted in running boards fouling station platforms while the trains were in motion'.

During an air raid passengers were expected to draw the blinds to protect themselves against flying glass. Stations were lit by dim blue lights and locomotives had a sheet to prevent the fire's glow being seen from the air. The sheet was agreeable enough in winter, but as it retained the heat in the cab it could make it unpleasantly hot. Many cases were experienced of heat exhaustion and heat rash. Engines with side windows had the glass removed and replaced with steel plates, otherwise the glow might have been seen from the air.

Carrying explosives by rail could be dangerous. On 2 June 1944, the eve of D-Day, driver Ben Gimbert and fireman Jim Nighthall were working a train of bombs destined for United States airbases in East Anglia. Approaching Soham, flames issued from one of their wagons, which had caught fire. Gimbert blew his whistle to alert the guard and gently applied the brake – a jerk could have exploded the bombs on the wagon and set off a chain of explosions.

He stopped 90 yards short of Soham station. Gimbert told his fireman to uncouple the burning wagon so that the locomotive could move it from the vicinity of homes. It was duly uncoupled and drawn towards open country. When it had travelled 140 yards, there was a fierce explosion. Nighthall was killed but Gimbert, despite being blown 200 yards, survived with injuries. Forty-four 500 lb bombs had exploded, reducing the station to rubble. Where it stood was a crater 15 feet deep and 66 feet across. If that wagon had not been detached, the whole town would have been destroyed. Both men were awarded the George Cross. The engine concerned, War Department 2-8-0 No. 7337, received little damage and was repaired, subsequently being sent to the Longmoor Military Railway and withdrawn in 1967.

Another exciting wartime event was when Yardmaster Rose at Temple Mills, east of London, discovered a raft of wagons set alight by a string of incendiary bombs. Thinking quickly, he arranged for a fire engine to be placed on an overline bridge, where it could jet water down on the wagons as they were propelled through by an engine.

In the two months before D-Day, the railways ran 24,459 specials, 3,700 of these in final week. Preston was a major troop train halt between Scotland and London and free drinks and sandwiches were offered to servicemen in uniform.

On 29 July 1944, a great drama was played out at Paddington. That summer, German V1 rockets had begun to rain on the capital and Londoners took the opportunity of their holidays to escape. Paddington became choked with thousands of potential passengers that Saturday but Government restrictions prevented extra trains being run.

Had a V1 fallen in the vicinity of Paddington that day, the number of casualties would have been unthinkable. The GWR made urgent requests to the Prime Minister's Office and sixty-three extra trains were permitted to be run to alleviate the situation. The V2 flying bombs were more devastating and gave no warning. An LNER J17 class 0-6-0 was destroyed by a V2 near Stratford and its crew killed. In Britain, during the Second World War air attacks on British railways killed about 900 people including 395 railwaymen and seriously injured 2,444, while nearly 3,500 railwaymen lost their lives after they had joined the services.

During the Second World War, the railways abandoned the practice of replacing old locomotives at the rate of approximately 430 annually; in fact, some engines already on withdrawal roads were returned to stock. Dean Goods 0-6-0s, an 1883 design, had seen War Department service in the First World War and in the Second World War a hundred were again required by the War Department. At Dunkirk, seventy-nine fell into German hands. The Railway Executive Committee ordered LMS Class 8F 2-8-0s, and 400 were built by all four of the railway companies. Although no other freight engines were allowed to be constructed, some railways were able to evade this ruling. The GWR managed to build more Hall class mixed-traffic 4-6-0s, and the SR the Bulleid Merchant Navy 4-6-2s, ostensibly for mixed traffic but really express engines. Some 935 Austerity class 2-8-0 and 2-10-0s were constructed, being a simpler version of the LMS Class 8F, with a steel firebox rather than a copper one. Built for use overseas, after the war they were taken over by British Railways.

In December 1942, the first of 756 American-built Class S160 2-8-0s arrived in Britain. Following the invasion of France in 1944, these engines were sent to the Continent. Before the invasion, 398 were loaned to British railways.

The different construction of these locomotives caused at least one fatality. At Honeybourne, just before midnight on 17 November 1943, the fireman of No. 2403, a Class S160 engine, was unfamiliar with the working of the steam valve to the water gauge and the fact that the gauge could show a false level in the glass if the valve was not fully opened. This led to the uncovering of the firebox crown, and its collapse fatally scalded the fireman. Although a conspicuous notice read 'This valve to be always in the open position', it was not appreciated that the valve was required to be *fully* open, and if only slightly closed would give a false reading. Unfortunately the valve spindle of No. 2403 was not opened fully as it was bent and so, unknown to the crew, was only opened as far as it would go.

To prevent a repetition of the accident, every plate was changed to 'this valve must be full open' and locomotive crews instructed why this was so important.

The first large convoy of US troops arrived in July 1943 and required eighty-six trains to convey them to camps in Britain.

Footplate crews and guards were always keen to work such trains, as when the troops detrained the crews were able to go through the coaches and pick up food items very scarce in Britain due to rationing.

One troop train caused havoc on the Somerset & Dorset line between Bath and Bournemouth. The servicemen failed to understand that hanging their kitbags conveniently on the emergency cord would bring the train to a halt. After several such stops, the guard politely informed a superior officer of the problem, which he failed to appreciate – the stops continued.

During the Second World War, the railways were Britain's lifeline because road transport was hampered by the fuel shortage and coastal shipping was attacked by the enemy; this meant that rail enjoyed an almost complete monopoly of transport. Between September 1939 and 11 August 1945, 538,559 special trains were run, of which 258,624 were troop trains and 279,935 were special goods trains.

As in the First World War, timber was in short supply. In response, the GWR experimented with concrete-pot sleepers, placing a concrete pot under each chair, the gauge being kept with tie bars linking opposite pots. These sleepers proved successful in sidings, particularly when laid on ash, which gave a better bearing.

As a wartime economy measure, thinner wood was used for wagon repair and open wagons were not repainted and relettered. An effort to speed up unloading and thus free wagons for another journey made use of volunteer labour at weekends to unload them. The volunteers were paid for their efforts.

A method of shortening the time a train needed to wait at a platform was to use female travelling porters. These were responsible for seeing that each parcel loaded went into the correct van and that the pile of parcels for each station lay by the most convenient door, ready to be unloaded. While the train was in transit between stations, the porter passed from van to van through the connecting gangways adjusting the stowage.

To fill the posts made vacant by railwaymen joining the forces, women were enrolled for such tasks as being porters, passenger guards, lorry drivers or engine cleaners, rodding boiler tubes to clear clinker; they also worked in railway workshops and were involved in track maintenance, and signalling. Women were not employed as goods guards as the brake vans had no toilet – a man could easily empty his bladder over the side of the van, but this facility was not available to a female. Many women opted for a job on the railways, this being much better than facing military discipline or the repetitive work necessary in munitions. By early 1943, 88,464 women were at work on the railways.

One lady signalman hung her handbag on the machine for issuing single-line tokens. The signalman at the next box, unable to withdraw a token, called out the engineer, who discovered that the weight of the bag had slightly drawn out the handle, rendering the machine inoperable!

Vans and coaches were converted into ambulance trains to cater for the expected casualties following D-Day on 6 June 1944; 14,743 trains were run to support the invasion, including 300 hospital trains. The latter were mainly worked by LNER Class B12/3 4-6-os, of Great Eastern design, which could travel over almost any line due to their relatively light weight. They were fitted with the Westinghouse brake. As they had to be prepared to go anywhere at any time, relief men lived on the train.

Some 160 prisoner-of-war trains were run in the first month to camps in Britain. To diminish the chance of escapes, signalmen were told to do their best to try and avoid stopping these trains at adverse signals.

Although the railways provided a vital service during the war, they did not benefit from it financially as fares and rates of charges were controlled to prevent inflation and government freight traffic was required to be carried at reduced rates. The railway companies did not receive the whole compensation for war damage. The government paid the Big Four, together with London Transport Passenger Board, a total of £43 million annually and pocketed the surplus £45,700,000 in 1942 and £62 million in 1943.

In addition to existing ports, the government opened secret new ones such as Cairnryan in Galloway, which eased congestion at Stranraer and Faslane on the Gareloch, serviced by a branch off the West Highland Railway. To improve wartime traffic flow, layout improvements were made in some areas. The GWR between Severn Tunnel Junction and Newport was quadrupled, as was Cheltenham to Gloucester; at Carlisle the bridge over the River Eden was doubled to offer two extra roads, while much of the Didcot, Newbury & Southampton line was doubled to cope with the anticipated D-Day traffic. The shell-filling factory at Thorp Arch near Harrogate required 18,000 workers and the LNER constructed 6 miles of track to the factory and dropped off the workers near their workplace.

As in the First World War, the railway workshops constructed war supplies for the government. Crewe designed and built Covenanter tanks, while other workshops also constructed tanks, guns, gun mountings, shells, bombs, aircraft components, Bailey bridges, midget submarines and landing craft, of which Eastleigh built over 260 and Swindon thirty-four. The railways constructed seventy-three firefighting trains. The LMS at Derby constructed twelve armoured trains.

Servicemen on leave travelled an average of 150 miles, which was twice the distance covered by an average civilian.

## 14

# Nationalisation; the Steam Railway Declines; Strikes; Closures

In the post-war period, the government had taken funds which should have been available for reconstruction after six years of hard usage and little maintenance. The government had promised before the war that, in the event of its outbreak, the companies would receive a reasonable share of the extra income earned by the increased traffic. However, the government reneged on its promise. As a Labour government had been returned in 1945, the only answer was nationalisation. Under the Transport Act of 1947, almost all British railways and canals were to be transferred to the British Transport Commission on 1 January 1948, together with road-haulage firms operating above a distance of 25 miles. The Big Four was divided into six regions: Eastern, comprising the LNER except for its lines in Scotland and north-east England; London Midland, with most of the LMS except for Scotland; North Eastern; Scottish; Southern and Western – the SR and GWR. British Railways had over 19,868 route miles served by a staff of over 700,000.

With hindsight, it would have made sense to continue building the best of the Big Four's steam engines until the main lines were electrified and carefully evaluate diesel propulsion, but the Railway Executive decided to embark on a new range of British Railways Standard steam locomotives, mainly for mixed traffic and covering all needs from light branch work to express passenger working. Nine types of two-cylinder simple engines were produced, and 999 built between 1951 and 1960. Time proved that it was especially foolish and wasteful to build small BR Standard class tender and tank engines for branch lines which were to be closed in the near future.

Existing engines were improved. The Castles were good machines, but locomotive development made them even better. Castles built in 1946 by Frederick Hawksworth, who had taken over from Collett in 1941, were given a three-row superheater instead of one with two-rows and in 1947 were fitted with one of four-rows. It proved such a success by reducing maintenance, prolonging boiler life and reducing water consumption that it became a feature of all future Castle and King class boilers. Some ten years later, both classes were given double chimneys and altered smoke-box draughting, while the final improvement was a new design of mechanical lubricator which delivered 50 per cent more oil.

Before the Second World War, a career on the railway was attractive as it was a job for life. But with the post-war employment situation, unless you were a lover of steam locomotives, the dust and dirt did not endear you to such working conditions. Vacancies for maintenance staff at locomotive sheds could not be filled, so locomotive performance suffered. Good steam coal was in short supply, which made a fireman's job more difficult and less attractive.

In May and June 1955, the Associated Society of Locomotive Engineers & Firemen struck to restore their differentials, which had been eroded. As in 1926, it was a short-sighted move as it encouraged passengers and freight to turn to the roads; the railway no longer held a monopoly.

The forties, fifties and sixties were great decades for collecting engine numbers. The Second World War brought 'foreign' locomotives to many lines – sometimes literally foreign, as when the USA-built 2-8-0s and 0-6-0Ts appeared in Britain just before the 1944 invasion of France, when they were sent to the Continent. Engine spotting was a marvellous free entertainment and, incidentally, a source of education. Quite apart from gaining engineering knowledge, there was the historical – the kings of England; the geographical – the countries of the empire; and natural history – the names of birds and flowers.

In 1955, the British Transport Commission was given money to embark on a Modernisation Plan. Part of the East Coast Route was to be electrified, as were lines from Euston to Birmingham, Liverpool and Manchester, along with some suburban services in north-east London and the Kent coast lines. Over the remainder of the system steam was to be replaced by dieselisation, using locomotives and multiple-unit railcars.

The freight side was to be developed by building new wagons, fitting the whole wagon fleet with continuous brakes and building – or rebuilding – over fifty marshalling yards. One great advantage of equipping wagons with continuous brakes was that goods trains could be speeded up, meaning that there was less likelihood of them delaying a faster train behind. Unfortunately, BTC opted to continue using the vacuum brake rather than the more efficient air-brake system. Within a decade the policy was changed; all new construction had air brakes, but the BTC still had large numbers of new locomotives and passenger and goods rolling stock with outdated vacuum brakes. Then, when freight trains were given faster schedules, derailments were caused by wagon suspension, which was not designed for such speeds.

One great failing of the Modernisation Plan was that it failed to anticipate future requirements and assumed needs would be as pre-war. The new DMUs (diesel multiple units) failed to win enough traffic from buses and the increasing number of private cars to cover their running costs. On the freight side, the railway strike of 1955 encouraged many firms to provide their own road haulage, which had the great advantage that it was reliable and not run at the whim of an outside party. Between 1958 and 1962, there was a 60 per cent increase in the number of lorries with an unladen weight over 3 tons. Although between 1958 and 1962 the volume of Britain's inland goods transport rose by 13 per cent, the railway's share fell by 12 per cent and the fifty new – or rebuilt – marshalling yards became redundant. BTC had not foreseen the situation we are in today, where rail freight is a complete *train*load and not a *wagon*load.

The BTC also overlooked inflation and the fact that increasing wages and salaries, together with increasing material cost, meant that railway income was insufficient to cover working expenses, leaving nothing to repay the cost of modernisation. There were many instances of overmanning.

Then dieselisation proved a problem. BR itself had little experience with such machines, and private British locomotive builders, which the government insisted that BR should use, had only produced small engines rather than those suitable for main lines. These British builders were anxious for their products to be run on BR so that it would provide a shop window for overseas buyers. Thus BR was landed with a plethora of various diesels that were unreliable and almost untried.

The BTC in the late fifties decided that, in order to try and control the dire financial situation, the answer would be to abandon steam almost immediately and go for rapid dieselisation. Thus in 1957 orders were placed for diesels which had not been evaluated; in time, some proved to have been the wrong choice. In December 1958, BR operated 16,108 steam locomotives, 105 main-line diesels and 2,417 DMUs. At the end of 1963, the figures were respectively 7,050, 2,051 and 4,145.

Then, in 1963, came the Beeching Report. Some routes were indeed uneconomic and needed to be closed, but there were marginal services which should have been retained because of the business they fed into the main lines. About 4,500 route miles were closed, 2,500 stations shut and 65,000 jobs lost. One good thing about the Beeching Report was that it stopped the inefficient use of wagons. An average wagon was loaded only once in twelve days, and then spent one and a half to two days completing an average journey of 70 miles. Coal left the pits in economic trainloads but then was split into wagonloads for individual merchants in various small yards. Beeching established mechanised concentration coal depots served by trainloads and then distributed by road to the surrounding area. He also proposed merry-go-round trains between coalmines and power stations. The hopper wagons used could be discharged automatically. One outcome of the many branch-line closures was that the modern light steam engines or DMUs built to work these lines were made redundant after just a few years' use. The investment in them had been wasted.

Then, at Swindon in 1960, BR built its last steam locomotive, Standard Class 9 2-10-0 No. 92220, and named it *Evening Star*, painting it in lined green livery rather than the plain black carried by its sisters.

The last main-line steam hauled expresses were those between

Waterloo and Bournemouth, and in the summer of 1963 the Bournemouth Belle was speeded to a two-hour timing for the 108 miles. Drivers of many of the expresses on this route took the opportunity of showing just what steam could do, topping 100 mph on occasions.

The Western Region intended to withdraw all its steam locomotives at the end of 1965, but then was thwarted for a few weeks when the Somerset & Dorset line had to be kept open until 7 March 1966. The last regular timetabled steam movement on BR was made by Class 5 4-6-0 No. 45212 on 3 August 1968. Steam was entirely withdrawn from BR on 11 August 1968, with the running that day of the Fifteen-Guinea Special from Liverpool Lime Street and back via the Settle & Carlisle line.

Class 5 4-6-0 No. 45110 took it from Lime Street to Manchester Victoria; Britannia class 4-6-2 No. 70013 *Oliver Cromwell* from Manchester to Carlisle Citadel; Class 5 4-6-0 No. 44871 and No. 44781 from Carlisle to Manchester; and No. 45110 back to Liverpool – a 315-mile round trip. This was actually not the last of BR steam, as it still continued on the 1 foot 11½ inch gauge Vale of Rheidol line.

This ending of steam traction meant that many steam engines were condemned which had years of use in them. Although at the time it was thought that the Fifteen-Guinea Special was to be the last main-line steam train, events proved this to be wrong.

E. S. Cox, in *Locomotive Panorama*, published in 1966, wrote,

Steam has had a very good run for its money, and has lasted far longer than it was reasonable to expect. It has so lasted because retention of the pure Stephensonian form in its successive developments produced a machine which for simplicity and adaptability to railway conditions was very hard to replace.

Research into the development of steam locomotives did not cease with the withdrawal of steam from British Railways in 1968. A triple-expansion engine working at a boiler pressure of 580 lb/sq. inch, as envisaged by Chapelon, would give a thermal efficiency of 19 per cent compared with 38 per cent for a modern diesel-electric. Should the cost of fuel per heat unit for steam become less than half that of diesel, a convincing case could still be made for steam, particularly as the public has a deep love of this form of traction. Burning a variety of clean fuels, footplate crews would work in clean conditions. As Jonathan Glancey wrote in *Giants of Steam*, 'The steam locomotive has always been far more than a machine. Warm-blooded by nature, it is a kind of living, breathing animal fashioned from metal.'

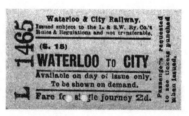

Waterloo & City Railway.
Issued subject to the L. & S.W. Ry. Co.'s
Rules & Regulations and not transferable.

(S. 15)

**WATERLOO** TO **CITY**

Available on day of issue only.
To be shown on demand.

Fare for single journey 2d.

Passengers requested
to see ticket punched
when issued.

L 1465

DISTRICT RAILWAY.
Available for day of issue only.

EARLS COURT (S.O.)

TO
Series 1

BRONDESBURY OR KILBURN

VIA WILLESDEN

6d SECOND CLASS 6d

Brondesbury or Kilburn    Brondesbury or Kilburn

SEE OVER

5528

Somerset and Dorset Railway.

# EXCURSION

TO

## DORCHESTER, via WIMBORNE,

FROM

_____30th of September, 1863,

Available to return same day.

*NOT TRANSFERABLE.*

15

# The Massive Preservation Movement

In 1865, the 2 foot 3 inch gauge Talyllyn Railway, 7 miles long, was opened to link Bryn Eglwys slate quarry to the port of Towyn, the line being opened to passengers the following year. The line was worked by two Fletcher, Jennings & Co. locomotives. In 1911, the quarry and railway were sold to Sir Haydn Jones.

With the rise of road transport, the line struggled to stay open and track maintenance left something to be desired. When Sir Haydn died in 1950, it seemed that the line would close. As it was still being worked by the 1865 engines, had a lot of character and was located in an area popular with tourists, O. H. Prosser suggested to author L. T. C. Rolt that a group of volunteers should be formed to run the railway.

Thus the Talyllyn Railway Preservation Society was established – the first of its kind. It raised funds and was able to reopen the line in 1951, since when a summer service has always been maintained. Over the years the preservationists have developed the line, still keeping its character, and have brought in additional locomotives and rolling stock.

Another narrow gauge line which narrowly escaped being lost was the 1 foot 11½ inch gauge Ffestiniog Railway. The introduction of buses to the district saw its passenger traffic declining, and after 1932 they were only operated in summer and withdrawn entirely at the outbreak of war in 1939. Slate traffic continued until 1946, and then the railway lay derelict.

In 1954, a group of preservationists secured control and, using volunteer labour, gradually reopened the line until they eventually reached Blaenau Ffestiniog again in 1982. The railway has its own works for locomotive building and maintenance and today the Ffestiniog is associated with the Welsh Highland Railway, which closed to passenger traffic on 26 September 1936, to goods in May 1937 and was lifted for scrap during in 1941. In an amazing renewal, the 25 miles between Caernarfon and Porthmadog have gradually been reopened through the heart of the Snowdonia National Park.

The Welsh Highland Railway uses the largest 1 foot 11½ inch gauge Beyer-Garratt locomotives in the world (they came from South Africa) to draw trains of modern, corridor-connected carriages with comfortable seats. The Welsh Highland Railway and the Ffestiniog Railway now form two of the principal tourist attractions in North Wales.

The success of the preservationists, attempting and succeeding in doing something never done before, gave inspiration for the film *The Titfield Thunderbolt*, filmed on the Limpley Stoke to Camerton standard gauge line just south of Bath. This line was unfortunately not preserved itself, but subsequently many standard gauge lines were, the first being the Middleton Railway and the Bluebell Railway, both in 1960. The former was an industrial line, which in 1812 had two rack-and-pinion engines designed by John Blenkinsop; these were the first railway engines in the world to be operated commercially.

Middleton was unusual for a preserved railway in that it

continued to carry daily goods traffic, whereas practically all other preserved railways rely on passengers. The volunteer Middleton Railway Trust was the first standard gauge preservation society to begin operation.

The Bluebell Railway is notable for the fact that it was the first British Railways branch to be reopened as a preserved railway. Throughout the years it has succeeded in extending its line, even digging out deep cuttings full of rubbish.

Some standard gauge lines were not preserved as such but have had narrow gauge railways constructed on their trackbeds, examples being the Brecon Mountain Railway and the South Tyndale Railway.

The 1 foot 11½ inch Lynton & Barnstaple Railway, closed in 1935, has been reopened for a mile or so west of Woody Bay station and the preservationists are hopeful of eventually reopening the line throughout. Some of the original coaches, preserved as summer houses, have been returned to railway use.

Railway equipment has been preserved for a much longer period. The Canterbury & Whitstable Railway's *Invicta* was preserved by the South Eastern Railway in the late 1840s. On the Great Western, the 2-2-2 *North Star*, the 4-2-2 *Lord of the Isles* and the 0-4-0T vertical-boilered *Tiny* were preserved, but the first two were cut up in 1906, leaving *Tiny* as the sole remainder.

The fact that no main-line broad gauge locomotive has survived led a group of enthusiasts to think of a rebuild, so a reproduction *Fire Fly* appeared. This has been followed by standard gauge creations such as the LNER Peppercorn class A1 Pacific No. 60163 *Tornado*. Similar projects are making new GWR Saint, Grange and County class 4-6-0s and an LMS Patriot class 4-6-0.

A Great Western steam rail motor was not preserved as such, but, when withdrawn in the 1930s, many had the boiler and driving bogie removed and were changed into auto coaches for locomotive push-pull working. As several of these have been preserved, the delightful idea arose of converting one back into a steam rail motor. This has now been achieved.

In the 1950s, British Railways restored a few of its historical locomotives back to steaming condition and ran them on special trains, some earning their keep by running ordinary trains in between. The 1968 ban on steam on British Railways after the withdrawal of its last steam engine terminated such outings, but BR relaxed its ban in 1972 and has since allowed steam excursions over some routes.

Another form of preservation is a steam centre. Instead of having a line with stations between which passengers can travel, a steam centre is basically an engine shed, or sheds, where locomotives can be restored and maintained and carry passengers on a short demonstration line. The Great Western Society's Didcot Railway Centre is an example of this. Apart from the sheds, there is a short standard gauge branch line, a short length of main line and a broad gauge line.

# Select Bibliography

Allen, C. J., *Railways of Today* (London: Warne, 1929)

Allen, C. J., *Royal Trains* (London: Ian Allan, 1953)

Bagwell, P. S., *The Railwayman* (London: Allen & Unwin, 1963)

Bulleid, H. A. V., *Master Builders of Steam* (Shepperton: Ian Allan, 1963)

Ellis, H., *The Trains We Loved* (London: Allen & Unwin, 1947)

Ellis, H., *British Railway History 1830-1876* (London: Allen & Unwin, 1954)

Ellis, H., *British Railway History 1877-1947* (London: Allen & Unwin, 1959)

Elton, A., *British Railways* (London: Collins, 1945)

Hewison, C. H., *Locomotive Boiler Explosions* (Newton Abbot: David & Charles, 1983)

Maggs, C. G., *A History of the Great Western Railway* (Stroud: Amberley, 2013)

Murphy, B., *ASLEF, 1880-1980* (Hampstead: ASLEF, 1980)

Nock, O. S., *The Railways of Britain* (London: Batsford, 1949)

Nock, O. S., *Speed Records on Britain's Railways* (Newton Abbot: 1971)

Perkin, H., *The Age of the Railway* (Newton Abbot: David & Charles, 1970)

Pike, J., *Track* (Stroud: Sutton, 2001)

Robbins, M., *The Railway Age* (Harmondsworth: Penguin, 1965)

Rolt, L. T. C., *Red for Danger* (London: The Bodley Head, 1955)

Simmons, J., *The Railways of Britain* (London: Routledge & Kegan Paul, 1962)

Simmons, J., *The Railway in England and Wales, 1830-1914, Volume 1* (Leicester: Leicester University, 1978)

Simmons, S., *The Victorian Railway* (London: Thames & Hudson, 1991)

Simmons, J. & G. Biddle, *The Oxford Companion to British Railway History* (Oxford: Oxford University, 1997)

Thornhill, P., *Railways for Britain* (London: Methuen, 1954)

Williams, F. S., *Our Iron Roads* (London: Bemrose, 1883)

# Index